Network based Teaching and Learning

Network based Teaching and Learning

R C Krishnamurthy

AUTHORSPRESS

Worldwide Circulation through Authorspress Global Network
First Published 2004
by Authorspress

E-35/103, Jawahar Park
Laxmi Nagar, Delhi-110 092

e-mail: authorspress@yahoo.com

Typeset in NewCenturySchlbk by Chitra Computers

Network-based Teaching and Learning
ISBN 81-7273-188-4

Printed in India at Tarun Offset, Delhi.

Preface

The rapid growth of the internet, and of the materials available online, offers great opportunity to make education more widely available and to enhance the learning experience of us all. The internet is bound to become an inseparable part of all the educational systems in the new millennium. In developed world it has already become an indispensable part without which the educational system can't function.

The net-based education system provides an integrated and distributed hypermedia information environment for the academic community. In this environment, instructors can construct course material and prepare some learning assistance for learners; learners can access course material and participate in online and off-line discussion using web browsers. The internet made the walls of the learning space transparent, providing freedom for the learner to explore sources of information outside his institution, even outside his country. It offers the potentials of thousands of classes on hundreds of subjects available any time night or day, at any place, at the convenience of the student.

The book is intended both as a broad review of ongoing and planned applications of the internet and its tools in education, and as an analysis of key technical and educational issues — as well as broader social issues — that these applications highlight. We hope that this book will stimulate discussions regarding the costs and benefits of net technologies in teaching and learning, the varied models these technologies offer for providing education, and the changing relationships between traditional institutions of education and a new generation of providers.

Editor

Contents

1

ICTs and Changing Venues of Teaching and Learning

The predominant technology being used for e-learning in the developed world is the world wide web, which in turn relies on the internet. At the end of 1999, more than 196 million people globally were using the internet; by the end of 2004, the number is expected to rise to 638 million.

There are many reasons for the rapid application of the web in education:

i) Through the use of browsers and a relatively simple programming language (HTML), the web provides universal standards and interoperability between different machines and operating systems, which allows for global reach and access.

ii) The web can be transmitted both through already-existing infrastructure, such as analogue telecommunications networks, as well as through high-speed digital networks, giving it a wide range of technical flexibility.

iii) The web is a low-cost technology for education for several reasons:

a) There is a relatively low cost of entry for educational suppliers. The cost of the technology needed for online courses is marginal compared with already-existing infrastructure costs for business and administrative purposes.

b) Development of materials is relatively low cost because of a simple computing language (HTML) for creating materials and the development of intermediary course authoring software that enables websites to be easily constructed.

c) Through its use of the internet, there is no direct charge for independent packets of information (as is the case with voice telephone calls); pricing is by volume (the size of the pipe into the institution), not by time or distance. Since most current applications use narrow bandwidths, the transmission costs per course for the supplier are virtually zero.

d) The web's ability to combine text, graphics and a limited amount of multimedia gives it a wide range of applications in education.

e) The web enables free and global access to a very wide range of high quality (as well as low quality) learning resources located on web sites.

f) The web offers opportunities for international, cross-cultural and collaborative learning.

g) The web enables learners to study at any time and, increasingly, from any place.

h) The web allows asynchronous (time-delayed) interpersonal communication, not just between instructor and student, but more importantly, between learners and other learners, through e-mail, bulletin boards and online discussion forums.

The ability to enable students to communicate with each other independent of time and distance moves distance education away from a transmissive, teacher-dominated model of education to a more interactive form of learning where students can adapt and apply learning to their own needs. In a knowledge-based society where information and knowledge are rapidly increasing, it is essential for students to be able to question, discuss and analyse their learning in a social context.

However, there are several constraints that limit even greater expansion of the web as a learning technology, particularly in developing countries:

i) In many developing countries, and in a small but significant number of communities and homes in developed countries, the necessary minimal technology infrastructure needed to support the web — a computer and a telephone simply do not exist.
ii) Even where the minimal infrastructure is in place, many people do not have the necessary computer, keyboarding and literacy skills to make effective use of the web.
iii) Most applications of the web still have to fit into narrow bandwidths, limiting educational materials to text and static graphics.
iv) To fully exploit the educational advantages of the web, teachers need to adapt and change their teaching methods. Without adequate support and instruction, teachers will merely add cost to the current system by bolting on the technology to traditional classroom methods.
v) Teachers also need technical support, both in terms of ensuring the networks, software and equipment work properly and are adequately maintained, but also in the design and development of web sites. This requirement adds substantially to costs.
vi) The interactive, participatory form of learning that has developed around the use of the web is culturally unsuited to the predominant mode of teaching and learning in traditional societies, which give great respect to the teacher, and where students are not expected to question the wisdom of elders.
vii) To justify the expense and stress of major changes in work methods, web-based learning needs to be used strategically and be adequately resourced. However, many administrations lack both the vision to use it for strategic change and the willingness to reallocate sufficient resources to ensure success.

New technologies have made the walls of the learning space transparent, providing a freedom for the learner to explore sources of information outside his institution, even outside his country. While ICT has undoubtedly opened new avenues for increased numbers of learners, it has also opened new areas of research focusing on the role of pedagogical processes when using new technologies and on their impact on cognition.

Kofi Anan, the United Nations Secretary General, has noted the broader impact of ICT, asserting that:

> Recent developments in the field of communication and information technology are indeed revolutionary in nature. Information and knowledge are expanding in quantity and accessibility. In many fields, future decision-makers will be presented with unprecedented new tools for development. In such fields as agriculture, health, education, human resource and environmental management, or transport and business development, the consequences could be revolutionary. Communications and information technology have enormous potential, especially for developing countries, and in further sustainable development.

The rapid development of virtual education is most noticeable in the developed world where there is much greater access to educational institutions and learning technologies, especially computers, CD-ROMs and the internet. In the developing world, limited access to ICT is apparent.

The internet access increases, in the corporate world, companies will focus on their ability to exploit internet and e-commerce opportunities. Employees will need to rapidly develop their knowledge and skills to use the technology and to redesign the business process. Many businesses will encourage in-house and distance education and training, and they will complement this with e-learning.

ICT makes it possible for many potential learners in many parts of developing countries, including remote and rural areas, to have access to education, such access is very limited. There are a number of technological constraints that restrict virtual education. For one, the telecommunications infrastructure (telephone and other communication facilities) outside many of the major cities in developing countries are limited and inadequate.

Another technology that is being used extensively in education is satellite broadcasting. Satellite television for educational purposes has a long history dating back to the early 1980s. India was one of the first countries to use satellite television through the INSAT project, and today Indira Ghandi National Open University is still a major satellite user.

Satellite broadcasting has the following features relevant to education:

i) Due to the relatively high infrastructure costs (studios, satellite transmission and receive sites), it has high fixed costs but very low variable costs; this makes it most effective when many students (usually numbered in thousands) can receive a single programme.

ii) It provides a common standard of lecture or teaching to all students, wherever they may be located.

iii) It fits a transmissive model of education, where students are expected to remember and understand what is being taught. Satellite broadcasting suffers however from the following constraints:

iv) It requires very high start-up costs and a high level of technical expertise to launch and maintain.

v) Despite the use of alternative technologies for two-way communications such as telephone and e-mail and the use of local teacher-supported discussion groups, it is difficult to make satellite broadcasting very interactive for learners.

vi) Learners with internet access have less flexibility in terms of time and place of study from satellite broadcasting than from studying through the web, being tied either to the time of the broadcast or to a fixed location if they do not have personal access to satellite reception equipment.

vii) The need to provide convenient, secure and accessible local reception sites can add substantially to the cost, especially for satellite TV. Satellite TV lacks the educational flexibility and the future potential for improvement that can be found in the web.

viii) Governments appear to be less willing to regulate and fund educational satellite TV initiatives, partly because of the high cost, and partly because of a move to more deregulated communications policies. In such a context educational users are usually unable or unwilling to pay full commercial rates for satellite transmission costs.

Satellite broadcasting has advantages for transmission of information to large numbers of students at relatively low cost per student. However, it needs strong local support on the ground, through local centres or alternative two-way communication channels such as telephone or the internet. These ground costs and the constraints on learning considerably reduce the economic and educational benefits of satellite broadcasting. Furthermore, well-designed printed texts can be more educationally cost-effective than real-time or even recorded satellite lectures.

Lastly, compact disc technology, in the form of CD-ROMs or digital video disk (DVD), is being used in a number of interesting ways in virtual education. These discs tend to be used for applications requiring large quantities of data in real time, such as multimedia applications. The discs can run on the student's local computer in conjunction with the web; the codes on the disc are accessed from a website, which can then call up images from the disk. Students can then seamlessly move between website and disk, thus overcoming many of the bandwidth constraints of the web.

The increased capacity of CD-ROMs and particularly DVDs facilitates a wide range of educational applications:

i) Large stores (databases) of slides, photographs or computer-generated images, each one digitally coded and catalogued, can result in the same CD-ROM being used in a variety of different courses.

ii) Video clips or learning objects often require too much time for downloading over the internet. Compression techniques now allow for high-quality video digital reproduction on CD-ROMs or the even greater capacity DVDs.

iii) Simulations enable students to enter data and see the consequences.

iv) A virtual lab can simulate many of the experiments and practices demonstrated in labs without the time required to set up experiments and equipment and with no worry about lack of convenient space. Expert systems, somewhat like games, can help students make decisions and see the consequences. The outcomes are governed by rules and procedures based on expert knowledge. Expert systems are valuable in facilitating decision-making in complex contexts.

CDs and DVDs are high-end educational applications of technology. While they indicate some of the possible future developments on a more universal scale over the internet, good-quality disc-based educational applications are very expensive to develop and require high skill levels. However, as more and more high-quality materials become available on discs, there will be opportunities for course developers to incorporate off-the-shelf discs into their own local programmes.

ICTs in Learning Process

To understand the potentials of ICT in education in a better way it is necessary to identify the key-elements of teaching and learning. A description of a conceptual model for the organisation of teaching and learning is given in this section. At the heart of this model we find the learning process. The learning process can be seen as a common key characteristic of teaching and learning in the past, in the present, and in the future. Given the central place of the learning process and the different ways in which it can be arranged, it is important to identify the driving forces behind this process.

There are four forces, representing two dimensions. These dimensions and forces are depicted in Figure 1.

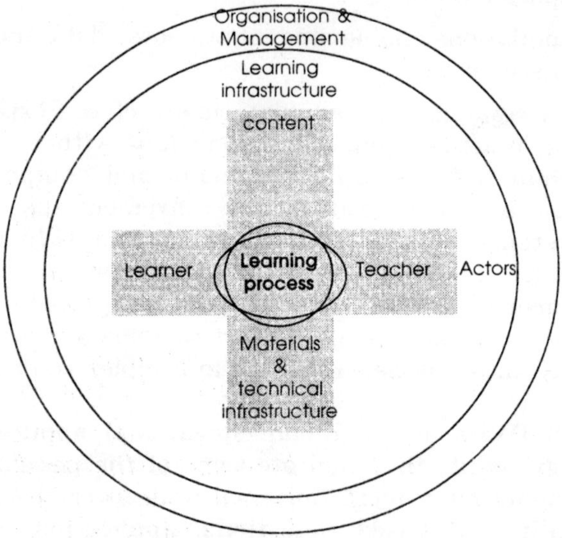

Figure 1. Driving forces behind the learning process

The horizontal dimension represents the relation between the actors in the learning process: the teacher and learner or student. The vertical dimension represents the learning infrastructure, consisting of content, teaching and learning materials and infrastructure.

The learning process takes place at the cross-section of these two dimensions, as a result of a balance between the four forces: teacher, learner, content and materials. The contribution at the level of school organisation and management on the arrangement of the learning process is represented by the outer circle. The figure illustrates the view that a learning process is the result of both structural conditions derived from the learning infrastructure and the personal characteristics of the actors involved, and their interaction.

Changing just one of the driving forces may lead to tensions, but not necessarily to substantial changes and improvement of the learning process. For example, providing schools with computers, software, and network facilities obviously changes the learning infrastructure in terms of availability of materials and technical infrastructure, but not necessarily the content of education or the roles of the actors in this process. Only in conjunction with changes in the roles of the teacher and the student, and with changes in the organisation of the content and corresponding curriculum materials is it possible to realise 'new' education and make use of the potentials such a new technical infrastructure holds for enhancing and renewing the learning process.

Learning always refers to a process in which the learner needs support in terms of well-adapted subject matter content, organisation of learning activities by a teacher, adequate materials and technical infrastructure. It is assumed that ICT has the potential to enhance such an approach of learning that not only prepares for but also suits the information society.

The role of the actors in the learning process (students and teachers), can be clarified by looking in more detail at the characteristics of the teaching and learning process in terms of concrete activities.

Table 1 provides an overview of the activities that can be distinguished in relation to the learning processes. The set of activities refers to three main categories of activities in the learning process: preparation, executing instruction, and regulation. In a traditional arrangement of the learning process most of the activities listed in Table 1 are under control of the teacher. If a learning process is more student-oriented it means, in operational terms of the activities listed in Table 1, that the student becomes more responsible for activities which are completely under control of the teacher in the teacher-oriented learning process.

The terms teacher-oriented and student-oriented refer to the actor who is most active and responsible for the arrangement of the greater part of activities belonging to the learning process.

Table 1. Activities in the learning process

I PREPARATORY ACTIVITIES

Cognitive

1. orientation towards learning goals and learning strategies
2. clarification of learning goals
3. choosing and defining subgoals
4. choosing and defining learning strategies
5. mobilising prerequisite knowledge

Affective

6. arousing students' curiosity
7. challenging students
8. generating interest
9. focusing attention
10. clarification relevance
11. getting under way

II. EXECUTING INSTRUCTION

12. absorbing knowledge, practising skills
13. reflecting
14. formulating conclusions
15. relating to what is being learned, getting an overview
16. conditions and possibilities for application

III . REGULATORY ACTIVITIES

Cognitive

17. testing progress and learning process
18. monitoring progress and the learning process
19. taking recovery actions
20. reflecting on the learning process and student progress
21. evaluating

Affective

22. controlling and regulating concentration
23. maintaining students' motivation
24. generating feedback
25. relating results to strategies used
26. self-assessment

There is no absolute distinction between both approaches because they indicate the opposite directions of a continuum. This means that both teacher-oriented approaches and student-oriented approaches have many different representations and that in an information society a new balance between the two is needed.

Society is in transformation toward the information and communication age. This future society will define its own institutions, such as education, anew. We can argue about the pace of change of society, be it evolutionary or revolutionary, but there is little room for debate that education and, even more, teacher training will need to change.

We can detect the future of education by carefully watching how the demands society puts to education are developing and how they are being met. These demands are serious and to a certain extent also overwhelming:

i) prepare students for the information age by giving them a solid education;

ii) contribute to the solution of problems such as isolation, ethnic integration, crime, non-labour, etc.;

iii) provide individualised, tailor-made and flexible education;

iv) provide opportunities for lifelong learning for everybody;

v) solve financial, managerial and organisational problems efficiently;

vi) prevent the occurrence of student-dropouts, in-school violence, teachers-absence, skipping of scheduled courses, teaching by unqualified teachers, and so on.

A shift from teacher oriented arrangements of the learning process towards more student oriented arrangements can be facilitated by ICT. However, until now these potentials of ICT have hardly been implemented. Most of the current ICT-applications are used to facilitate the teacher-oriented arrangements of the learning process.

Applications of ICT are adapted to the existing teaching routines; the beliefs and attitudes of teachers towards their teaching practices did not change, and basically the teaching and learning process itself did not change. The use of ICT as a substitution of the current teaching and learning activities can be seen as the first of three phases through which the implementation of new technologies generally diffuses.

Ways of ICT use in Education

During the past years many ICT applications have been developed for educational purposes. Most of these applications reinforce the existing teacher-oriented instructional practice and some refer to new instructional methods. There are various ways ICT has been used for educational purposes. Looking at ICT as part of the learning process, a distinction can be made in three different forms: ICT as object, as aspect or as medium. In addition ICT is often used as a tool for organisation and management in schools. In the latter case ICT is not integrated in the actual learning process but supports it at classroom level or even at school level.

ICT as an Object

The use of ICT in education as an object refers to learning about information technology and is mostly organised in a specific course such as 'computer education' or 'informatics'. As an object, ICT has been broadly implemented in the curricula of schools, especially in secondary education. Following the 'ICT-as-object-courses', students familiarise themselves with the most important ins and outs of information technology as a dominant phenomenon in society. Its educational aim is prevention of computer illiteracy. At present, education is quite good at this. The easiest way to meet the challenge of technological revolution is to create and implement a new subject, so that the existing subjects do not have to change.

ICT as an Aspect

ICT as an aspect refers to specific applications of ICT in education as used in industry, business and professional practice. Such a use in education is for the most part found in vocational education, for example, in the training for computer-aided design and manufacturing, and computer-mediated accounting. Vocational training in these areas is unthinkable without ICT integrated in it. ICT as an aspect also appears outside the vocational territory, in subjects that are no longer teachable without the technology. For example, in general secondary education, carrying out experiments in science education, or accounting as part of economics. For that reason ICT has become an obligatory part of the general exams in science and economics in general secondary education in the Netherlands. The educational aim of ICT as aspect in education is job preparation. Today, ICT as object and as aspect are firmly embedded in our educational practice.

ICT as a Medium

Using ICT as a medium refers to ICT as a tool for teaching and learning itself, the medium through which teachers can teach and learners can learn. ICT as medium appears in many different forms, such as in drill and practice exercises, in simulations, in tutorials, in individual learning systems (ILS), in educational networks, in hypermedia programmes, in tests-generating systems, etc. We speak of ICT as a medium whenever ICT is used to support the teaching and learning process and not specifically its content. Despite the variety on different kinds of ICT applications, current practices of actual use of ICT as medium are few, though there is a growing interest in applications of ICT.

The use of ICT as medium in the learning process in the educational field for which teachers need to be prepared, implies that ICT should be an aspect of the teacher profession. At this moment, ICT as aspect in teacher training is hardly developed, obviously because it is only used as replacement of existing practices. Apart from that, it is hardly used in the daily practice of teachers, other than as replacement of existing practices such as paper and pencil exercises. Consequently, the use of ICT as a medium to enhance the teacher training seldom takes place.

Nature of Learning Venues

The development of information and communication technology (ICT) and its application to education and training have increasingly allowed institutions to deliver learning in a variety of venues. Now, the choice of venue is driven by, among others things, the ability to access the learning materials using ICT. Many potential learners do not have ICT in their homes, so there is a need to find alternative ways to access such learning experiences. Institutions using ICT as the delivery platform for learning can be defined as virtual institutions.

Enrolment in all sectors of the education system has increased in recent years. It is estimated that "two trillion dollars or one-twentieth of global gross domestic product" is spent on education. Roughly speaking, one-fifth of this amount is being spent by the private sector while the rest is spent by governments on the public education system. International and national campaigns such as "education for all" have succeeded in drawing learners into the education system, but the development of distance education opportunities has also had much to do with the growth in numbers. Research conducted by the International Data Corp indicate that "distance learning enrolments are growing by 33 per cent and will reach 2.23 million in 2001." Many students are attracted by the prestige of offshore degrees, and this trend it likely to continue as distance and virtual education continue to develop.

The world is changing rapidly in all areas—in the environment, in the economy, in technology and in education. While it is important to spend time pondering the implications of such change, perhaps it is more important to consider the implications of the changes to education. The education system should be the key platform that enables young people to develop the necessary skills required to prepare for the changing world.

The introduction of ICT to support virtual education has generated a range of discussion, generally focusing on the value of using the technology for this form of education delivery. Often such discussion illustrates a lack of unanimity on the issues that need to be addressed for the effective use of technology to support virtual education. However, there are three issues that seem to generate consensus by all people involved in education: costs, decision making and access. The COL study on virtual institutions noted that the lack of access to learning venues and the lack of access to connectivity and learning technologies within venues was a major constraint, particularly in developing countries. And it is this element of education, the "place" of the educational interaction, that is increasingly being seen as crucial to promoting access to virtual education.

In focusing on learning venues, a range of vital questions should be considered to guide the thinking on the spatial and social construction of such venues. These include:

i) What are the implications for learning where students are able to access second opinions and further information to that provided by the textbook and teacher? How can the student access such opinions and information, and what technology will best serve this purpose?

ii) What will the role of the teacher be in the context of different learning venues and environments? When does the teacher become the author, the expert, the tutor, the presenter and the facilitator? What learning space is required to enable the teacher to carry out these tasks?

iii) Increasingly there is a shift away from a class defined only by age to individually tailored education based on the requirements of each student. Using resource-based methods, institutions are able to cater to different students in terms of their capabilities, potential and stage of learning maturity. What are the implications of this for peer group relations, teachers, tutors and librarians? What are the implications in terms of the nature of the learning venue and its physical construction and its resources?

iv) Shifting away from mass groups of students to individual learning requires administrative and resource control systems that enable such learning to occur. What are the implications of this type of system for the learning space necessary for the learner to be successful?

Such questions pose interesting considerations on the nature of the learning structure. The "building" may be a school; or part of other public buildings like libraries, town centres, community centres; or part of private buildings like shops, factories or telecentres. In constructing such "buildings," issues such as noise, connected and unconnected spaces, electricity and telecommunications, and public and private learning spaces need to be considered.

Learning Centres

A community learning centre (CLC) is a site where education programmes that are relevant to the needs of the community are made available to the members of the community. These centres are located in different types of buildings (e.g., public buildings, religious buildings, community halls, public schools). The key characteristics of community learning centres are "flexibility, responsiveness to local needs and the creative and efficient use of available resources and infrastructure." CLCs are often connected to various data sources and networks and use these connections to offer various opportunities such as:

i) Offering services and resources based on local education and training needs.

ii) Providing access to formal and non-formal training and skills development programmes.

iii) Being a catalyst for communities to make use of their own resources.

iv) Providing information and communication according to community needs.

v) Acting as access points for local and outside resources.

vi) Providing a base for community development forums.

Of late, a new term, "telecentres," has been derived to describe a centre that offers various communication services. Telecentres are communal facilities consisting of a physical space that provides public access to ICTs for educational, personal, social and economic uses. The services offered range from basic telephony, fax and e-mail to full internet connectivity.

Basic telecentres are generally small operations that are either privately owned or run by non-governmental organisations (NGOs) as part of their services. The NGO operation is often funded by international donor agencies.

Basic telecentres are usually found in rural, marginalised or peri-urban areas that support poor communities with high levels of illiteracy. They usually offer "a mix of services including telephony, fax, computing, internet, photocopying and related technologies." As well, they often have a small number of computers that use dial-up connections to an internet service provider (ISP). The key to the success of basic telecentres is that they are linked to the local community they serve and their workers are drawn from the local community.

Telecentre franchises refer to a number of interconnected telecentres that are independently owned. As they are based on a franchise model, there is a centrally located organisation that facilitates technical and/or financial support.

The cyber cafe model is one that needs further exploration as most are based on a for-profit basis. However, the rapid growth and popularity of cyber cafes, especially in urban areas, is worth noting and exploring ways for their use to support access to virtual education opportunities. Some community-oriented cyber cafes offer preferential rates or services to communities or local organisations while still maintaining their commercial business activities to the general public.

In India, the MS Swaminathan Research Foundation has partnered with the International Development Research Centre (IDRC) to implement the Information Villages Research Project in the Pondicherry region. This project is based on the argument that providing information and adding value to such information is vital to enabling rural families to access it. The project has established value-added centres where staff scans the internet for information on technologies, health, transport, public events, education, subsidies, prices of local commodities, etc. Thus the value-added centre acts as the hub site and uses VHF radio system for a local area network that connects the hub to village information centres.

Each shop varies in the way it is operated and supported. One has a village development council; another has a non-formal trust established by the community; a third uses space allocated to it by the locally elected panchayat. The shops each have a pentium PC with multimedia software and printers. The PC is connected to the wireless network through a modem. Each shop also has a board to display bulletins and other village information. Given the range of information available via the hub site, various members of the village use the shop for different purposes.

Clearly the need for education and training is the main driving force for the development of innovative learning venues. As noted earlier, there has been a massive increase in the number of students enrolled in various sectors of the education and training system.

There has also been increasing demand for professional development opportunities that has resulted in the rapid increase in the number of private sector providers using technology to deliver education and training. This growth, coupled with the developments in ICT, has resulted in learning being accessed in creative ways. The concern to bridge the digital and information divide is also an important driving force in the development of innovative learning venues.

With the drive for learning comes the need for individually tailored education that notes a person's capability, potential and level of maturity in terms of his or her own learning progress. This need for individually tailored education has been helped by the development of resource-based learning, distance education and, more recently, the creation of learning objects for content aggregation. Enabling the individual learner to access education opportunities using ICT has ensured that there is an emerging market for education. This in turn has driven the development of innovative access points to learning opportunities.

Access is not only about hardware and software; it is about creating an environment which attracts students by providing them with a place to meet their peers and teachers/tutors and with access to resources necessary to complete their courses. The need for more physical space in the form of traditional classrooms is often resisted in developing countries because of the cost.

The strength of being able to access learning at all times can also act as a constraining force. By increasing access to the technology, greater demands are placed on the time of the tutor or instructor. These demands are for quick responses to queries, assignments and other work for assessment, for keeping the website updated and for electronic discussions. This requires proper planning, both for the network that is being used to engage with students and with the response time for feedback to students.

The rapid development of virtual education has brought to the fore different challenges to the provision of education and training. The delivery of virtual education, that is the provision of an educational transaction for a formal certificate or for non-formal purposes, has shown tremendous growth and is likely to increase as the demand for education and training grows. However, this growth and projected increased demand has been and is likely to be uneven with the developed world being able to fully exploit the advantages of virtual education. The developing world, with its difficulties in education systems, education processes and practices, infrastructure, telecommunications infrastructure, lack of ICT infrastructure, etc. will constantly find itself at the lower end of usage of virtual education. To encourage access, the development of innovative learning centres has been occurring. Such developments have been experimental in nature and driven in large part by development agencies and the private sector. These centres face crucial challenges in terms of their sustainability, their effective management and meeting their target group's needs. Despite these challenges, such centres offer access to learners of various virtual education opportunities. The development of these centres need to be encouraged and supported if they are to be effective in ensuring that more learners are able to take advantage of virtual education opportunities.

The development of a learning/multipurpose centre requires certain issues to be addressed and structures to be in place:

i) The physical location of the centre needs to be in a community to enable easy access for users.
ii) The start-up process must ensure that there is a clear understanding of what the centre is going to do and the needs that it will be meeting.
iii) The mission must be clear and focus on identified needs that are being expressed by the various user groups within the community.
iv) The structure of the centre in terms of its organisational requirements (including staff, management structures and procedures, financial systems, etc.) and infrastructure (including the appropriate ICT) must meet the varied needs of the community. Community support must be achieved through a mixture of assessing needs, marketing the services and functions, working with community structures and involving such structures in the governance of the centre.
v) Appropriate links and partnerships with different service providers must be created.
vi) These should include education and training institutions, various NGOs, small and micro enterprises, all levels of government, etc.
vii) Needed services and functions must be delivered.

Such services and functions need to meet the needs of the community being served as well as the internal needs of the centre. (Internal needs include management training, financial and resource management, evaluation and ongoing needs assessment.) However, such centres should not be seen as the only means to enabling access to virtual education and training. Clearly these centres need to be encouraged as part of a series of strategies that encourage learners to access virtual education, including learning in the home, workplace and elsewhere.

ICTs in Education: Current Trends

Knowledge and information have become the most important currency for productivity, competitiveness, and increased wealth and prosperity, nations have placed greater priority on developing their human capital. Governments around the world are thus focusing on strategies to increase access to and improve the quality of education. Today's information and knowledge-driven world, a whole new set of skills is required.

A relevant education is more important today then ever, because today's networked world demands a workforce that understands how to use technology as a tool to increase productivity and creativity. These skills include "information reasoning", a process in which reliable sources of information are identified, effectively accessed, understood, contextualised, and communicated to colleagues. Furthermore, employers require workers to have the skills necessary to collaborate, work in teams, and share information across global networks, that is, to analyse issues from a multidisciplinary perspective. Since these networks are international, employers seek out individuals who have the capacity to effectively interact with others across fullcultures and languages.

The knowledge workers need to be flexible and able to learn quickly as work environments continue to change dynamically. Workers must learn how to learn, and quickly acquire new skills. In 1997, the World Bank initiated the World Links programme in response to developing countries' demand for strategies to prepare their youth to compete in a world increasingly driven by information, technology, and knowledge. World Links is one of the most innovative and successful grant programs initiated by the World Bank to assist developing countries in bridging the "digital divide."

Its principal capacity-building objective is to provide developing country schools and ministries of education with sustainable solutions for mobilising the necessary technologies, skills, and educational resources to prepare students and teachers to enter the networked world.

Over the past four years, World Links has worked with 21 countries to bring underprivileged schools into a global school network. The network links thousands of students and teachers around the world for collaborative learning and helps ministries of education pilot and learn from this implementation of Networked Learning in schools. World Links is bridging the gap in skills, knowledge, and educational opportunities between students in industrialised and developing nations, as well as between rich and poor students within developing countries. In developing its programme, World Links drew lessons from the successes and failures of technology education programmes throughout the world and designed customised pilots for each participating country.

Since World Links launched its first programme in Uganda almost five years ago, a number of lessons regarding the constraints, as well as the potential of integrating technology into education in the developing world, have been learned. While getting schools wired to the internet is the first step, a whole host of other factors need to be considered, ranging from teacher training to assessment to sustainability.

In a recent survey of teachers in developing countries conducted by SRI International for World Links, the majority of teachers in African and Latin American countries reported that the lack of adequate hardware and software as well as unreliable internet access were significant barriers to using computers in instruction. Many schools in developing countries have a student-teacher ratio as high as 80:1, and must contend with a computer lab of 10 to 20 computers for the entire school—if they are lucky.

Moreover, most schools with computers can only afford dial-up connectivity, which in many cases runs over old lines and antiquated telephone exchanges. With this level of connectivity, a lab with 10 to 20 computers in Uganda is like a fire hose dangling over a thirsty traveller in the desert that releases only drops of water into his parched mouth. There are many limitations for these labs work.

Schools squeeze as much use as possible out of poor connectivity through technical solutions such as store-and-forward e-mail, caching web pages locally, extensive use of CD-ROMs, and pulling web pages through e-mail. Teachers have also learned to manage their classes to work with these limitations. Many teachers divide their classes into groups to allow some students to work off-line while others use the computer to either search for information, input information, or create information for a project. Existing computer technology is still not appropriate in terms of complexity and cost for a school environment—particularly in a developing country. Cheaper, easier-to-use technology must be developed and implemented in schools to allow for greater use among students and teachers.

Most schools lack the funds for a full cultures time computer technician, and when one is hired and trained, he is often lured away to a more lucrative job elsewhere, leaving the school to start the search over again. Moreover, most ministries of education are ill equipped to effectively service a large number of schools. Most schools are therefore left with very little technical support when inevitable technical glitches arise. However, a few innovative solutions have emerged in countries around the world. One solution is to give students more responsibility for maintaining the labs. Many students are as or more adept with the technology than the "professional" technicians who are often hired.

Emerging wireless technologies is another regulatory area that needs attention. Since reliable fixed line connectivity is still mostly limited to only urban areas in developing countries, wireless options are attractive to rural and peri-urban communities. As wireless technologies continue to develop and become more ubiquitous, however, governments need to evaluate their spectrum allocation and licensing policies to ensure that satellite connectivity options allow for a broad range of choices for the connection of underserved areas of the country.

World Links has found that the most effective technology for connecting schools in developing countries is wireless. Developing country schools are now bypassing their local fixed line infrastructure and establishing wireless internet access. In Uganda, there is a telling case of the schools' evolution to broader band internet connectivity using wireless solutions. Lack of financing is one of the greatest challenges to connecting schools in developing countries to the internet.

Governments need to form strategic partnerships if they are to succeed. India presents a wonderful example of an effective partnership between the public and private sectors. A number of states in India have implemented a variation of the community learning centre concept by partnering with private sector computer training companies.

While many ministries of education around the world have made the commitment to computerise schools, few have developed coherent strategies to fully integrate the use of computers as pedagogical tools in the classroom. One of the significant bottlenecks that World Links has encountered is the lack of a clear policy in ministries of education with regard to use of computers in education. Many ministries of education view computers as a stand-alone subject requiring a curriculum focusing on basic computer literacy skills.

While computer literacy represents a start, the integration of computers and the internet into the broader curriculum is where real learning gains will be made. Computers by themselves bring very little to the learning process—they are only tools, like many others. Linking computers and the internet to learning objectives is a challenging goal, but is one of the most important that education policy makers can achieve.

If our education system is to meet the challenges of the information society, it means an increasing need for learning situations responding to flexibility (adaptability to different needs), accessibility (learning when and whenever suits best) and support (an adequate learning infrastructure to assist learners). If this learning process has to change according to the needs of the information society, it does not merely mean a change in terms of putting technology in the classrooms; it means finding a new balance between all driving forces behind the learning process. In a traditional, mostly teacher oriented educational setting the teacher is completely responsible for the arrangement of most of the learning activities.

If the current education system wants to meet the challenges of the information society, it is inevitable that the role of the teacher has to change and the student has to become more actively involved in the learning process. It is assumed that ICT is an adequate medium to support the shift from teacher-oriented towards more student-oriented ways of learning. Although it is uncertain to what extent this shift will take place and how much time this will require, the direction of future change is clear: the learner will become more responsible for the arrangement of his or her own learning process. Characteristic for such a learning process is that it responds to flexibility, accessibility and support. It is assumed that ICT can facilitate a learning process that meets these characteristics.

It is the task of the teacher training institutes to anticipate these developments and to prepare teachers for these new roles. In other words, teachers have to be prepared for a new balance between student oriented and teacher-oriented arrangements of the learning process. Even though flexibility, accessibility and support become the key issues of the education of the future and the students become more active, the teacher will continue to play a key role in the learning process. Teachers need to be trained in designing and organising such innovative teaching and learning environments because they continue to be the key actors in the teaching and learning process.

The major question for the future is not whether education can be delivered online or will be supported by multimedia, but what is the best mix of didactical approaches to achieve the goals of education within the constraints of the available resources and characteristics of the students. This means that the challenge is not getting technology and computers into schools but integrating information and communication technology into the teaching and learning process in order to improve the learning outcomes.

Potential advantages of using ICT for the teaching and learning process are, for example, that ICT can help students learn at their own pace, provide them with unlimited sources of information, offer access to other learners and mentors which can be motivating for students of all ages.

Using ICT as a learning medium offers students the opportunity to learn to collect information, organise their thinking, give meaning to information, revise their work, collaborate on projects with others, and present knowledge to audiences. These skills are relevant for students who have to be prepared for the information society in which one of the most important tasks is to handle information. Each student can not only proceed at his/her own pace but can also take certain responsibilities for learning as an active participant. The relevance of these possibilities become more important with the ageing of students; with optimal utilisation in upper secondary and higher education.

ICT allows the student to focus on real problems, make connections to different fields of interest and construct their own knowledge. In such an approach the teacher's role is one of an adviser and a facilitator, arranging the conditions for learning.

However, many schools do not make the most of the benefits of technology. One of the problems is that the school buildings are designed for the teaching and learning process belonging to the industrial era. Another problem is that teaching and learning in a technology enriched learning environment asks for new roles of teachers, new roles of the learner and an update of curriculum contents. But even in schools in which classrooms have all the characteristics of modern communication centres for learning, the basic tool of instruction continues to be the blackboard and chalk. It is clear that teachers must have more time and opportunity to integrate ICT into the curriculum before schools can benefit from technology.

Recent studies show that a majority of teachers feel inadequately trained to use technology and are not aware of how ICT can improve learning or help them to improve their job. It is assumed that a new understanding of how we learn will result into several shifts in teaching methodology:

i) from whole-class to small-group instruction;
ii) from lecture and recitation to coaching;
iii) from working with better students to working with weaker students;
iv) from assessment based on test performance to assessment based on product, progress and effort;
v) from competitiveness to cooperation;
vi) from all students learning the same things to different students learning different things;
vii) from the primacy of verbal thinking to the integration of visual and verbal thinking.

Studies in the field of the implementation of technology in education show that many teachers go through identifiable stages on their way to become experienced technology users. In the early stages they use computers to support traditional methods of teaching, such as drill-and-practice, text orientation, whole group lectures and seatwork. Later on, as teachers gain confidence, they use technology as part of more innovative instruction, including team teaching, interdisciplinary project based instruction, and individually paced instruction. Finally, they enter an inventive stage in which they experiment and change using, technology to support active, creative and collaborative learning. It is this process that ultimately results in the shifts in teaching methodology that were described above.

In order to prepare student teachers for future education, the current teacher training institutes should shift their focus from serving the current education (teacher oriented) to serving what emerges as the education of the future (student oriented). Teacher training institutes have to create both space and opportunities in their programme for such a transformation. This causes a dilemma because teacher training institutes cannot refrain completely from providing the current education system with teachers that can function in the existing situation.

The solution for this dilemma is to distinguish a transition period first, covering the timespan from our current situation to the situation in which education will get its new shape. This implies strengthening the development of something 'new', while 'old' still exists. During the transition process 'old' needs care and attention, but should not prevent 'new' from growing. 'Old' should be challenged to 'emerge into new', but at the same time, 'new' needs stimulation and incentives. Thus, the transition period can be summarised in terms of both 'care' and 'courage': care for the existing practices and courage to explore and start new arrangements of the learning process.

The development of new practice is a matter of participation of all relevant partners in the process. This means that teacher training institutes will have to establish and maintain close relations with teachers and students of primary and secondary education. The mutual exchange of new approaches for learning has to become a natural 'attitude' within the education system.

Threats of ICT Implementation

There are also a number of potential problems or possible threats related to the integration of technology in the teaching and learning process. Such problems and threats could be a reason for refraining from the process of educational change and ICT-integration. However, refraining from the developments will ultimately result in even larger problems. Being aware of the potential problems and threats should make us more conscious in elaborating our plans and strategies so that we can avoid these to happen.

Pressures limiting the use of ICTs

Despite the very strong pressures on educational institutions to use ICT, there are other strong pressures that limit its use.

Perhaps the most important and least appreciated is the newness of the phenomenon. The world wide web did not exist as a public service before 1990. The first web-based educational course did not appear until 1995. The web and the internet are disruptive technologies. They require a fundamental rethinking of teaching practice. Students no longer are required to be at a set time and a set place to learn. Teachers are no longer the gatekeepers of knowledge. At the same time, schools, colleges and universities play a much wider role than merely transmitting information from one generation to another. They have social and cultural roles as well. Therefore educators are right to be cautious before rushing to adopt the latest technology. Education needs to match the needs of learners. Technology should be used only if and when it contributes to those needs.

Secondly, any move towards using new technologies requires significant up-front technical investment, even if for other commercial reasons the basic national infrastructure already is in place. Most public institutions, even in the richest developed countries, are under-invested in this area. As a consequence, the technology is often not conveniently available, is unreliable and requires a high level of competence and skills on the part of the teacher and often the students to use. Ironically, the inefficiencies caused by under-investment often cost more than properly investing in the first place. Nevertheless, even a well-planned investment requires initial additional spending from government and/or the institutions.

Thirdly, most institutions have not provided adequate support and training for teachers to use the technology appropriately in an educational setting. As well as technical support, teachers need help with media production and instructional design. Without this, the use of technology is just bolted onto existing practice.

Lastly, because the application of the web to teaching is so new, there are very few convincing research and evaluation studies that indicate clear educational benefits for such an investment. Evidence is beginning to emerge, though, and the picture is not entirely positive.

Ethical issues

The use of computer networks can change everyday classroom practice in a drastic way. Interaction through networks connects students and teachers with the outside world. Until now, the teacher was the most important gatekeeper in school who controlled the degree to which the outside world could enter daily classroom life. In 'traditional' educational settings teacher control for this is only limited when it comes to student use of the library. Access to a computer, a modem and phone lines frees students from the physical limits and time constraints of a library and a school environment.

Networking allows students to send electronic mail, participate in computer conferencing, and access information from remote sources. In that sense, the outside world may get a larger influence on the teaching and learning process. However, the prospect of students having open access to unrestricted materials is a matter of great concern to many parents, educators, and community members. Many believe that children should be protected from being exposed to or having the opportunity of finding inappropriate information. It is clear that the internet has not been designed with children in mind and therefore many potentially difficult issues still need to be discussed.

Legal issues

Today, technological and legislative changes that have been enacted by the information society threaten to disrupt the delicate balance, which has been struck between the rights and interests of individuals, industries, and societies. Copyright is expanding with regards to the items protected, but also with regards to the area and the period of protection. Industry is moving quickly to secure the distribution of their products. The copyright distributors use new contracts and technological devices for the protection of their goods.

New technological barriers to the public domain have emerged along with different electronic management systems. These tools make it possible to licence access and to monitor online utilisation of works with contractual and technological protections. In many countries, notably in Europe and the United States, the copyright period has been extended from 50 to 70 years after the creator's death. The increased emphasis on profit has affected the development of ICTs for education; legal negotiations have resulted in the General Agreement on Trade in Services (GATS) and the agreement on Trade-Related Intellectual Property Rights (TRIPS) under the GATT/WTO negotiations. The GATS is an important step in a process of 'opening' markets for services and the Millennium Round of GATS negotiations is expected to 'bring forward' the debate on the privatisation of education.

Only 40 of 143 member-states of WTO have agreed to fully implement GATS in the field of education. The GATS is therefore not fully operational in the field of education, but its implementation is indicative of the trend towards international competition in national education markets. The TRIPS relates to educational goods, and includes technology-related intellectual property such as computer software. Computer software areas protected under TRIPS include the prohibition of exact or near-exact copying of programme code and certain aspects of user interfaces.

Some developing countries express more interest in technology transfer than in the encouragement of domestic innovations and appropriating new technologies. The fundamental premise of private property rights in industrialised countries—that knowledge is a private capital—is challenged by a number of developing countries. It was argued that in some countries certain forms of intellectual property are viewed as a public good and that some cultures are hostile to any notion that knowledge is a private capital.

The TRIPS and GATS legal agreements explicitly open the doors for multinational companies to fill education market niches and to compete with traditional institutions. The integration of ICTs and education is becoming both a key factor for global economic success and a big business in itself. The private sector is very interested in getting a larger share of what it calls the education market, where global public spending tops one trillion dollars. This figure represents the costs of over 50 million teachers, one billion pupils and students and numerous educational establishments.

Education businesses (for-profit schools, publishers, school supply companies, corporate training firms, etc.) generate nearly US$100 billion in revenue annually. There is, however, a notable lack of reliable information concerning the scope and growth of this education market, particularly with regard to the e-learning market. This phenomenon is largely explainable by the fact that hardware, software, training and telecommunication companies, corporate consulting firms, start-ups, franchises, etc., have an important financial interest in forecasting exponential growth in this field. These groups tend to present the complete technological makeover of education as a matter of urgency.

Traditionally, the state assures the financing, provision, administration, and regulation of educational activities. In principle, the advantages of this system of 'education as a public good' are: equitable access to education; quality education for all (through the redistribution of resources, coherent methodologies and the harmonisation of curricula etc.); the promotion of civic responsibility and a common set of values (education that empowers people to contribute effectively to the democratic development of the country); and the preservation of cultural diversity.

Nevertheless, public education systems are often hampered by difficulties in realising their full potential due to factors such as: severe budgetary constraints affecting quality and access; long-term planning objectives maintained by rigid, top-heavy bureaucratic structures that restrict the provision of uptodate ICT training options; and lack of a clear strategy for linking national education policy objectives to global challenges arising from international diplomatic negotiations.

Ideally, private industry would be capable of providing custom tailored 'just-in-time' education based on good analysis of industry needs. It could primarily facilitate online education content mobility and access to the latest technologies. In the past, private providers have also improved teaching quality in certain programmes through the training and evaluation of teaching staff as well as the recruitment and support of part-time staff with both practical and teaching expertise. However, greater involvement of private industry in education brings risks that threaten the main objectives of public education systems.

Limited resources and lack of competition between suppliers may adversely affect quality, access, and price of educational services, as marginalised groups do not constitute a significant 'target' market. In addition, the objective of private companies is not to develop autonomous, critical future citizens, but workers and consumers. New e-learning providers are not bound by the norms and ideals of traditional higher education and thus might fail to link research and teaching, and to provide community service, a comprehensive curriculum, or academic autonomy and control.

A serious risk of using public funding to support national education and ICT development is that it may only nurture an illusion of egalitarianism, while differences in access to computer communication in fact reinforce existing inequalities within the countries. Though private industry, motivated by the growing ICT and education market, has the means to counter difficulties faced by public education systems in specific fields and to contribute to the improvement of services, it might also weaken the last inclusive fortresses, which form critical citizens on all levels education systems.

Social issues

Integration of ICT in the learning process, and especially of internet, will influence patterns of communication and interaction between students in a classroom, and therefore the learning 'culture'. A possible threat is that the interaction between students, needed for the development of social and communication skills, be replaced too much by student-machine interaction. Teachers and teacher students need to learn to recognise, analyse and assess the new learning environments on this potential threat and to learn that the use of ICT is sufficiently embedded in 'social learning'.

Issues of accuracy

Internet is a huge decentralised network with information changing literally from minute to minute. The use of internet for both professional development and instructional purposes requires constant accommodation to rapid change and tolerance for ambiguity. Going online in the classroom implies that the teacher is no longer the authority having all the relevant knowledge available; the teacher becomes a co-learner. This adds to the difficulty of teaching teachers the skill of using internet. Different conditions of access to the net and different purposes for using it greatly affect the choice of an appropriate training model for teachers to get acquainted with this network. The quantity of information on worldwide networks like internet is staggering and finding the necessary information in a quick and efficient way is becoming more and more difficult. It seems necessary that effective filters become available to help teachers and students to find accurate and uptodate information.

Issues of effectiveness, accessibility and equity

Many schools do not have the means to judge the effectiveness of software programmes and resources in increasing student achievement before purchase. Besides, the use of educational software by students at home is heavily skewed to higher income families. If students at schools do not have the opportunities to benefit from ICT's motivating possibilities for the acquisition of knowledge, skills and attitudes, this can cause a new area of inequity.

Issues of teacher training

The professional development of teachers sits at the heart of any successful technology and education programme. Teachers need not only formal training, but also sustained and ongoing support from their colleagues to help them learn how best to integrate technology into their teaching. Training must go well beyond basic cutting-and-pasting. Teachers need to be able to transform their classrooms from places where a static one-way flow of information from teacher to student occurs, into dynamic, student-centred learning environments in which learners interact with peers in teams, both in their own classroom as well as with virtual classes around the world through the internet.

Most teachers, however, are intimidated by technology and are comfortable with their own teaching styles. Any teacher training programme should help teachers see past the technology to the pedagogical and educational gains that use of the technology will bring to the classroom. Furthermore, teachers need to be transformed from information consumers, using the internet to access resources, into information producers, adapting the information for their particular cultural and educational reality. Some countries have established online networks or communities-of-practice, in which teachers share resources that enhance their curriculum, get peer reviews of lesson plans they have created, and exchange ideas and good practices with other teachers of their subject.

Technology as a tool for teachers to transform their classrooms into interactive, inquisitive learning environments. When schools are connected to the internet, teachers taught to rethink their teaching methods, and students empowered to use technology, the impact can be profound. Teachers quickly see how the use of computers energises the students and makes the classroom a more interactive learning environment.

References

Bitter, G. G, Yohe, R. L., "Preparing teachers for the information age", *Educational Technology,* 29 (3), 22-25, 1989.

Boaz, Mary, et al., *Teaching at a Distance: A Handbook for Instructors*, Los Angeles, CA: League for Innovation in the Community College and Archipelago, a Division of Harcourt Brace & Company, 1999.

Boettcher, Judith V, and Rita-Marie Conrad, *Faculty Guide for Moving Teaching and Learning to the Web*, Los Angeles, CA: League for Innovation in the Community College, p.16, 1999.

Brown, A. L., "The advancement of learning", *Educational Researcher*, 23 (3), 4-12, 1994.

Chaurasia, Gulab, *Teacher Education and Professional Organisations,* Authorspress, New Delhi, 2000

Kulik, J. A, and Kulik, C.L., "Effectiveness of Computer- based Instruction", *School Library Media Quarterly*, 17, 156-159, 1989.

Lave, J, Wenger, E., *Situated learning: Legitimate peripheral participation*, Cambridge, UK: Cambridge University Press, 1990.

Pachler, N., *Theories of Learning and ICT* ed. Marlyn Leask and Norbert Pachler, London: Routledge, 1999.

Pascarella, Ernest and Patrick Terenzini, *How College Affects Students*, San Francisco, CA: Jossey-Bass, 1991.

Peters, Otto, *Teaching and Learning in Distance Education: Analysis and Interpretations from an International Perspective*, London: Kogan Page Limited, 1999.

Twining, "Planning to use ICT in schools?", *Education* 3-13, Vol 29, Issue 1, pp. 9-17, 2001.

2

Instructional Strategies for Active Learning

All learning is inherently active and students are therefore actively involved while listening to formal presentations in the classroom. To be actively involved, students must do more than just listen: they must read, write, discuss, or be engaged in solving problems. They must engage in such higher-order thinking tasks as analysis, synthesis, and evaluation. Strategies promoting active learning is defined as instructional activities involving students in doing things and thinking about what they are doing. Use of these techniques in the classroom is vital because of their powerful impact upon students' learning.

Some cognitive research has shown that a significant number of individuals have learning styles best served by pedagogical techniques other than lecturing. Therefore, a thoughtful and scholarly approach to skilful teaching requires that faculty become knowledgeable about the many ways strategies promoting active learning have been successfully used across the disciplines.

The modification of traditional lectures is one way to incorporate active learning in the classroom. Discussion in class is one of the most common strategies promoting active learning—with good reason. If the objectives of a course are to promote long-term retention of information, to motivate students toward further learning, to allow students to apply information in new settings, or to develop students' thinking skills, then discussion is preferable to lecture.

To achieve these goals the faculty must be knowledgeable of alternative techniques and strategies for questioning and discussion, and must create a supportive intellectual and emotional environment that encourages students to take risks. Several additional strategies promoting active learning have been similarly shown to influence favourably students' attitudes and achievement. Visual-based instruction, for example, can provide a helpful focal point for other interactive techniques.

In-class writing across the disciplines is another productive way to involve students in doing things and thinking about the things they are doing. Two popular instructional strategies based on problem-solving model include the case study method of instruction and guided design. Other active learning pedagogies worthy of instructors' use include cooperative learning, debates, drama, role playing and simulation, and peer teaching.

But certain specific obstacles are associated with the use of active learning including limited class time; a possible increase in preparation time; the potential difficulty of using active learning in large classes; and a lack of needed materials, equipment, or resources.

"Learning strategies", or "instructional strategies" are the various methodologies used to involve the learners in the training programme, such as questioning during lectures, simulation with CBT, reflection after reading, etc. They are used to obtain the "learning objectives" which are the new behaviours that you want your learners to use when they return to their jobs. The learning objectives, in turn, point you towards the major avenue of "media" (plural of medium), in which you will present your instruction, such as through the use of CBT (Computer-Based Training), self-study, classroom, OJT (On-the-Job Training), etc. Although many people use the terms interchangeably, objectives, media, and strategies all have separate meanings.

Active Learning Strategies

The methods and approaches of active learning include:

Table 1. Learning Theories and Instructional Strategies

	Behaviourism	*Cognitivism*	*Constructivism*
Representations of the Learning Process	Stimulus-response Reinforced behaviour Antecendent behaviour Consequence Sequenced knowledge and skills presented in logical limited steps	Cognitivist learning perspective Information processing schema Mental models	Inquiry-based Discovery learning
Relevant Frameworks	Programmed instruction (Logical presentation of content, overt responses, immediate knowledge of correctness)	Events of instruction (Conditions of learning)	Cognitive Apprenticeship Cognitive Flexibility Situated Learning Zone of Proximal Development
Key Principles	Learning happens when a correct response is demonstrated following the presentation of a specific environmental stimulus Emphasis is on observable and measurable behaviours	Learning is a change of knowledge state Knowledge acquisition is described as a mental activity that entails internal coding and structuring by the learner.	Learners build personal interpretation of the world based on experiences and interactions Knowledge is embedded in the context in which it is used (authentic tasks in meaningful realistics settings)

(Contd...)

(Contd...)

		Learner is viewed as an active participant in the learning process	
		Emphasis is on the building blocks of knowledge(e.g. identifing prerequisite relationships of content)	Create novel and situation-specific understandings by "assembling" knowledge from diverse sources appropriate to the problem at hand (flexible use of knowledge)
		Emphasis on structuring, organizign and sequencing information to facilitate optimal processing	
Goal of Instruction	Communicate or transfer behaviours representing knowledge and skills to the learner (does not consider mental processing)	Communicate or transfer knowledge in the most efficient, effective manner (mind-independent, can be mapped onto learners)	Build personal interpretations the world based on individual experiences and interactions (constantly open to change, cannot achieve a predetermined, "correct" meaning, knowledge emerges in relevant contexts)
	Instruction is to elicit the desired response from the learner who is presented with a target stimulus	Focus of instruction is to create learning or change by encouraging the learner to use appropriate learning	Learning is an active process of constructing rather than acquiring knowledge strategies

(Contd...)

(Contd...)

	Learner must know how to execute the proper response as well as the conditions under which the response is made Instruction utilises consequences and reinforcement of learned behaviours	Learning results when information is stored in memory in an. organised, meaningful way Teachers/designers are responsible for assisting learners in organizing information in an optimal way so that it can be readily assimilated	Instruction is a Process of supporting knowledge construction rather than communicating knowledge Do not structure learning for the task, but engage learner in the actual use of the tools in real world situations
Instructional/ Learning	Behaviourism instructional cues	Information processing model	Modelling Collaborative Learning
Strategies	To elicit correct response Practice paired with target stimuli Reinforcement for correct responses Building fluency (get responses closer and closer to correct response)	Explanations Demonstrations Illustrative examples Gestalt theory Matched non-examples Corrective feedback Outlining Mneumonics Dual-coding theory Chunking information	Coaching Scaffolding Fading Problem-based learning Authentic Learning REALs Anchored Instruction Cognitive Flexibility Hypertexts Object-based Learning

(Contd...)

(Contd...)

Multiple opportunities/	Repetition
trials (Drill and	Concept mapping
practice)	Advanced Organisers
Discrimination	Analogies
(recalling facts)	Summaries
Generalisation	Keller's ARCS model of motivation
(defining and	Interactivity
illustrating concepts)	Synthesis
Associations	Schema theory
(applying explanations)	Metaphor
Chaining (automatically	Generative learning
performing a	Organisational strategies
specified procedure)	Elaboration theory
	Links to prior knowledge

i) Collaborative learning
ii) Cooperative learning
iii) Discovery-based learning
iv) Engaged learning
v) Problem-based learning
vi) Whole language approach

Collaborative Learning

Collaborative learning is an educational approach to teaching and learning that involves groups of learners working together to solve a problem, complete a task, or create a product. It is based on the idea that learning is a naturally social act in which the participants talk among themselves. It is through the talk that learning occurs.

There are many approaches to collaborative learning:

— Learning is an active process whereby learners assimilate the information and relate this new knowledge to a framework of prior knowledge.
— Learning requires a challenge that opens the door for the learner to actively engage his/her peers, and to process and synthesise information rather than simply memorise and regurgitate it.
— Learners benefit when exposed to diverse viewpoints from people with varied backgrounds.
— Learning flourishes in a social environment where conversation between learners takes place. During this intellectual gymnastics, the learner creates a framework and meaning to the discourse.

In the collaborative learning environment, the learners are challenged both socially and emotionally as they listen to different perspectives, and are required to articulate and defend their ideas. In so doing, the learners begin to create their own unique conceptual frameworks and not rely solely on an expert's or a text's framework. Thus, in a collaborative learning setting, learners have the opportunity to converse with peers, present and defend ideas, exchange diverse beliefs, question other conceptual frameworks, and be actively engaged.

Collaborative learning strategies

There are mainly four types of collaborative learning strategies. They are:

i) *Think-pair-share*: (a) The instructor poses a question, preferably one demanding analysis, evaluation, or synthesis, and gives students about a minute to think through an appropriate response. This "think-time" can be spent writing also. (b) Students then turn to a partner and share their responses. (c) During the third step, student responses can be shared within a four-person learning team, within a larger group, or with an entire class during a follow-up discussion. The calibre of discussion is enhanced by this technique, and all students have an opportunity to learn by reflection and by verbalisation.

ii) *Three-step interview*: Common as an ice-breaker or a team-building exercise, this structure can also be used also to share information such as hypotheses or reactions to a film or article (a) Students form dyads; one student interviews the other (b) Students switch roles (c) The dyad links with a second dyad. This four-member learning team then discusses the information or insights gleaned from the initial paired interviews.

iii) *Simple jigsaw*: The faculty member divides an assignment or topic into four parts with all students from each learning team volunteering to become "experts" on one of the parts. Expert teams then work together to master their fourth of the material and also to discover the best way to help others learn it. All experts then reassemble in their home learning teams where they teach the other group members.

iv) *Numbered heads together*: Members of learning teams, usually composed of four individuals, count off: 1, 2, 3, or 4. The instructor poses a question, usually factual in nature, but requiring some higher order thinking skills. Students discuss the question, making certain that every group member knows the agreed upon answer. The instructor calls a specific number and the team members originally designated that number during the count off respond as group spokespersons. Since no one knows which number the teacher will call, all team members have a vested interest in understanding the appropriate response. Again, students benefit from the verbalisation, and the peer coaching helps both the high and the low achievers. Class time is usually better spent because less time is wasted on inappropriate responses and because all students become actively involved with the material

Conditions for effective collaborative learning

There are three key conditions for effective collaborative learning:

— Group composition
— Task features
— Communication media

Group composition: One factor that determines the efficiency of collaborative learning is the composition of the group. This factor is defined by several variables: the age and levels of participants, the size of the group, the difference between group members, etc. Regarding the number of members, small groups seems to function better than large groups in which some members tend be 'asleep' or excluded from interesting interactions. Most of the mechanisms described in the previous section, e.g., mutual regulation, social grounding, shared cognitive load, can only occur between a few participants. This does not argue in disfavour of large group sessions. It simply means that distance learning activities should also include 'closed' sessions, in which a restricted number of subjects collaborate and/or 'monitored' session in which the teacher takes care that no learner is left out the interaction. Regarding the participants, some developmental level is necessary to be able to collaborate, but this is only an issue for children and does hence not directly concern current distance education activities which mainly concern adult learners.

The most intensively studied variable is the heterogeneity of the group. It refers to the objective or the subjective differences (how subjects perceive each other) among group members. These differences can be general (age, intelligence, development, school performance, etc.,) or task specific. Results indicate there exists some 'optimal heterogeneity', i.e. some difference of viewpoints is required to trigger interactions, but within the boundaries of mutual interest and intelligibility. Heterogeneity can easily be understood as a condition to trigger conflicts and require social grounding, two important mechanisms described above. Heterogeneity is also implicit in the socio-cultural theory and its related mechanisms (internalisation and appropriation) which rely on the observation of adult-child pairs or at least pairs with one member being more knowledgeable on the task than the other.

Internet-based information and communication tools have a great potential with respect to heterogeneity: no infrastructure can better cross geographic, cultural and professional boundaries. Nevertheless, human beings have a natural trend to assemble with those who are the most similar to them. When participants join the group on their own decision, there is no control of heterogeneity. If the tutor observes too much homogeneity among the group members, he may modify some conditions in order to activate anyway the mechanisms that normally rely on heterogeneity. He may for instance allocate role to participants which will inevitably create conflict or provide them with contradictory information.

Task features: The effects of collaboration vary according to the task. Some tasks prevent the activation of the mechanisms described above, while other tasks are appropriated. For instance, some tasks are inherently distributed and lead group members to work on their own, independently from each other. Interaction occurs when assembling partial results, but not during each individual's reasoning process. Without interaction, none of the described mechanisms can be activated. Some tasks are so straightforward that they do not leave any opportunity for disagreement or misunderstanding. Some tasks do not involve any planning and hence create no need for mutual regulation. Some tasks cannot be shared, because they rely on processes (e.g., perception) which are not open to introspection or on skills (e.g. motor skills) that leave no time for interaction.

If distance teachers want to take these features into account, a first attitude would be to use only collaborative learning for tasks for which it will get its optimal efficiency. Another solution is to modify the task, as explained in the previous paragraph, to make them more suited for collaboration. For instance, the 'jigsaw' method consists of providing group members with partial data. This method artificially turns a monolithic problem into a task which requires collaboration. Task features also include the environment in which the task has to be performed. This is especially important in computer-based tasks. The software features may modify interactions among learners. For instance, if a computer-based task provides the learner immediately with a feedback on their actions, it may prevent them to discuss the consequences of their action

Communication media : Whatever task and group members have been selected, the collaboration may not work because the medium used for communication is not adequate. It would be beyond the scope of this paper to describe each available media. Basically, most of current widely available internet-based tools use text-based communication, synchronous or asynchronous, with mostly fixed graphics and images. Voice and video interaction or voice and video mail are of course available, but the overload of standard networks and the limits of currently available hardware has postponed their larger use in current distance education.

Most of the mechanisms described in the previous section can be conveyed via text-based communication, but with some perturbations. For instance, the cost of interaction being higher with text, the group members may reduce the number of disambiguating sub-dialogues used in social-grounding. At the opposite, in asynchronous text messages, they have more time to build sentences which are less ambiguous. Without video link, members also loose facial expressions which are useful to monitor the partner's understanding. Even with video images, they may see their partner but ignore where the partner looks, something which is important for understanding what she refers to. Some video system support eye contact with appear to be related to metacognitive aspects.

Benefits of collaborative learning

Collaborative learning:

— Develops higher level thinking skills.

— Promotes student-faculty interaction and familiarity.

— Increases student retention.

— Builds self esteem in students.

— Enhances student satisfaction with the learning experience.

— Promotes a positive attitude toward the subject matter.

— Develops oral communication skills.

— Develops social interaction skills.

— Promotes positive race relations.

— Creates an environment of active, involved, exploratory learning.

— Uses a team approach to problem solving while maintaining individual accountability.

— Encourages diversity understanding.

— Encourages student responsibility for learning.

Cooperative Learning

Cooperative learning is a successful teaching strategy in

which small teams, each with students of different levels of ability, use a variety of learning activities to improve their understanding of a subject. Each member of a team is responsible not only for learning what is taught but also for helping team-mates learn, thus creating an atmosphere of achievement.

Documented results include improved academic achievement, improved behaviour and attendance, increased self-confidence and motivation, and increased liking of school and classmates. Cooperative learning is also relatively easy to implement and is inexpensive.

Cooperative learning strategies

Here are brief descriptions of a few learning strategies.

Roundtable: It is a technique used for brainstorming or reviewing. Groups are seated around a table with one pencil and one piece of paper. A question is posed, and students take turns recording answers on the paper as it is passed around the table. The question should be carefully chosen. It should have multiple answers, and students should be capable of answering it. When time is called, teams count their responses written on the paper. Answers are then shared and validated by the entire class. Teams should share their successful strategies before going on to another round. Variations of this technique include rewarding the group with the most complex or complete answers.

Numbered heads: Students are arranged in teams of three or four, and each individual is assigned a number. Groups are assigned a learning task and given time to accomplish it. Everyone is encouraged to learn the material because one group member is later called on randomly to answer for the group. A question is posed, and the number of a student is then called. This student is responsible for the answer. Variations of this strategy include the collection of only one answer sheet when written assignments are completed collectively.

Talking chips: This is a method of providing opportunities for all members of a group to participate in a discussion. In order to talk, a student must place a chip (a pen will do) in a central area. Students cannot talk a second time until pens from everyone are placed in the centre. This technique assures that all students have an opportunity to comment on the topic.

Three-step interview: Students in groups of four first work in pairs. One student interviews or questions another. Student then switch roles with the interviewer becoming the one interviewed. Findings are shared among the group of four in a "round robin" fashion. This technique may be used when introducing a new topic. Questions such as, "What do you already know?", "What do you want to learn?", and "How can we do this?" increase student awareness and motivation.

Here are some typical strategies that can be used with any subject, in almost any grade, and without a special curriculum:

i) Group investigations are structured to emphasise higher-order thinking skills such as analysis and evaluation. Students work to produce a group project, which they may have a hand in selecting.

ii) STAD (Student Teams-Achievement Divisions) is used in grades 2-12. Students with varying academic abilities are assigned to four or five-member teams in order to study what has been initially taught by the teacher and to help each reach his or her highest level of achievement. Students are then tested individually. Teams earn certificates or other recognition based on the degree to which all team members have progressed over their past records.

iii) Jigsaw II is used with narrative material in grades three-12. Each team member is responsible for learning a specific part of a topic. After meeting with members of other groups, who are "expert" in the same part, the "experts" return to their own groups and present their findings. Team members then are quizzed on all topics.

Cooperative learning programmes

Some of the successful cooperative learning programmes that use specially developed material include:

— *Team accelerated instruction (TAI) in mathematics*: An elementary, individualied programme that provides direct instruction within a cooperative learning setting, emphasising concepts, real-life problems, and manipulatives.

— *Cooperative integrated reading and composition (CIRC):* A comprehensive approach to reading and writing/language arts for grades two-six that integrates the latest reading research findings with the essential components that make cooperative learning so successful.

— *Success for All*: A schoolwide programme for grades pre-K through five that strives to ensure that every child will be performing at grade level in reading, writing, and math by third grade and will be able to maintain grade level from then on.

— *Finding out/Descubrimiento:* A science and math curriculum for bilingual Spanish-English students in grades two through five.

Schools are using similar strategies with both students and teachers to do the following:

— Develop and use critical thinking skills and teamwork;

— Promote positive relations among different ethnic groups;

— Implement peer coaching;

— Establish environments where academic accomplishments are valued; and even

— Cooperatively manage schools.

Many studies have demonstrated cooperative learning's effectiveness on a range of outcomes:

— *Student achievement*: When two necessary key elements—*group goals* and *individual accountability*—are used together, the effects on achievement are consistently positive.

— *Improved relations among different ethnic groups*: One of the earliest and strongest findings shows that students who cooperate with each other like each other.

— *Mainstreaming students with learning disabilities*: Significant improvements in relationships occur between these students and other children in their class when these learning strategies are used.

Discovery-based Learning

Discovery-based learning is based on the belief that students do better when they figure things out for themselves.

Discovery-based teaching is the active teaching of concepts through self-reinforcing questions. Each question, and each lesson, is a link to the next question and next lesson, with each link becoming a stepping stone on the path to learning.

Courses with discovery-based content, help students focus their existing knowledge. We then add to their knowledge, not by simply presenting more information, but by getting students discover new information for themselves through more guided questions. In the end, students have so absorbed the information that it really seems they knew it all along.

Well-designed and motivating cases are essential to effective discovery-based learning. So too, are skills related to effective problem solving and decisionmaking. But there is a third, and irreplaceable ingredient, for a complete case-based learning experience: discovery teaching.

Discovery teaching is a process by which the instructor creates an inquiry-based learning context, or environment, in which learners, through active engagement with the content, the instructor and other students, "discover" the meaning, power and application of ideas.

The dominant objective in content-based teaching is to accomplish "coverage"; to get a lot of content across by following a detailed lecture or presentation plan. In the discovery approach, the objective is to change the learner's behaviour or upgrade his/her performance by improving thinking, problem solving, creative and analytic skills and competencies. In the discovery model, the role of the instructor is to be an "arranger of experiences", a facilitator, a catalyst and a moderator.

The teaching styles in the two approaches are dramatically different. The didactic style is based on direct, uninterrupted transmission of content to the learners. In the discovery style, the emphasis is on Socratic interchange and group learning processes.

The questioning style is also different in the two approaches. In the didactic style of instruction questions, when they are posed, are often the "checking form" of questions deployed to verify whether learners understood the content of the lecture. In the discovery approach, questions provide the engine of the learning process eliciting ideas and concepts from learners. In the discovery model, a range of different types of questions are deployed for a range of learning purposes.

The role of the learner in the lecture mode is passive, absorbing and digesting information. In the discovery classroom, the role of the learner is active and involves the process of constructing and giving meaning to the ideas and information in the case and the ensuing discussion.

Here again there are significant differences between the two approaches. In the lecture mode, feedback from the learner is used primarily to assess understanding and retention. In the discovery approach, feedback from the learner is used in the process of group construction of knowledge and to examine the capacity to apply knowledge to case situations.

Importance of Questioning

Central to discovery teaching in case based learning, as noted above, is the process of questioning which can be initiated by both the student and the instructor. Under the guidance of the instructor, cases are interrogated, collaboratively analysed, mutually extended and otherwise examined in depth and breadth. A key instructional skill, in this context, is the art of questioning. In case-based learning, as in other learning situations, there are effective and ineffective types of questions. Good questions, in case-based learning, tend to share the following characteristics:

i) *Brevity*: Long, wordy, and windy questions tend to overload learner's "intake valves". They often create confusion. Keep your questions lean and short.

ii) *Clarity:* Each question should focus, or zero in, on one point only. Overly complex and multi-faceted questions, while they may provide a way for the instructor to display his "brilliance", will often produce intimidation and frustration and forgetfulness of each part, not thoughtfulness.

iii) *Pertinence:* The question should be targeted to the theme or issue in the case, which is being discussed. In this regard, there is no substitute for pre-preparation by the instructor.

iv) *Challenge*: Good questions are those that provoke thought and encourage evaluation, analysis, synthesis and creativity. Questions which merely exercise a learner's "memory bank" should be used sparingly. In regard to questions that "challenge", there are six types which have been shown to be particularly powerful in case based learning:

a) *Convergent:* These questions challenge the learner to bring together facts or concepts to form other facts or theories. For example: "Based on the behaviour illustrated in the case, what principles of work motivation can you develop?"

b) *Divergent: These* types of question evoke interpretation, explanation and translation. For example: "How would you explain the reluctance of the firm to abandon yesterday's star products in the face of a decline in market sales?"

c) *Application*: These types of question press the learner to apply what has been learned in one case, or a part of a case, to other cases or the real world. For example: "To what extent do you think that the strategy behind the success of Software Co. could be applied to revive Hardware Computers?

d) *Evaluative*: These types of questions require that the learner enter into the process of making judgments about the facts presented in the case and the actions of actors in various situations.

e) *Perceptual*: These types of question ask the learner to place himself in the role of one of the people in the case situation and examine the world from that perspective.

f) *Lateral*: These types of question ask the learner to look at the case situation in new and novel ways as a means of spurring their creative processes.

In using discovery teaching, within a case-based learning process, the instructor approaches the case discussion with an inquiring mind, that is open to new insights and concepts that often flow from the discussion itself. It is important to remember that, in case-based learning, there are no absolute solutions to problems, that are presented. For this reason, one can say that case-based learning develops the ongoing knowledge and skills of the instructor, as much as it does those of the learner.

Active listening

While using effective questioning strategies to engage learners is central in case-based learning, so too is providing a context in which learners are attentive to the discussion that ensues in case exploration. Listening, in other words, is equal in importance to talking in case-based learning, both for the instructor and the learner. Many communication problems emerge in case-based learning settings, because listening skills are ignored, forgotten or assumed to be in operation. People often confuse hearing with listening. Hearing is picking up sound vibrations, while listening is making sense out of what we hear. Listening requires paying attention, interpreting and remembering incoming information. Another myth, that surrounds the notion of listening, is that effective listening is a passive activity.

Effective listening, however, is an active process. It requires that a person empathise with the speaker, in order that he can understand the communication from the point of view of the speaker. Active listening is hard work and entails skills, that can be learned through practice. Central to discussions of cases, then, is the capacity to listen to the viewpoints being expressed by others. This applies both to the instructor facilitating case based learning as to the learners who engage in the process.

Research has shown that there are four basic ingredients to active listening: intensity, empathy, acceptance and a willingness to take responsibility for completeness.

Mutual learning, through the mutual engagement of minds and experiences, is at the heart of the teaching process in case based learning. And these processes are generated through the combined impact of: one concentrates intensely on what the speaker is saying and tunes out the distractions, and other noise, that diverts this attention.

Intensity involves summarising and integrating what is being said in the context of what preceded it. Empathy requires that a person be able to put himself in the shoes of another person, in order to understand what the speaker wants to communicate, rather than what you want to hear or understand.

Empathy, or role-taking, requires knowledge of the speaker and flexibility on the part of the listener. It also requires the capacity to suspend judgement, that is to demonstrate acceptance, and the tendency to rush toward interpretation.

The final component of active listening involves taking responsibility to ensure that what was said by the speaker was heard, as the speaker intended, and to probe until that match is achieved. The process of verification entails asking questions to the speaker to ensure that there is a correspondence between what is intended and what is received in a message.

Active listening in case based learning can best be facilitated by the instructor demonstrating the skill in the context of the learning process and coaching the learners in active listening through the case discussions. In this regard, there are a number of techniques which can be used to create a climate within which active listening flowers:

— *Be motivated*: In order to hear what the other person is saying you first must make the effort. Active listening is hard work and requires a commitment to sustain it.

— *Make eye contact*: People often judge whether you are listening to them by looking at your eyes. One way to generate a feeling that you are actively listening to someone is to make eye contact with him or her.

— *Empathy*: Do not project your own needs and intentions into the mind of the speaker. Ask yourself, who is this speaker and where is he coming from? What are his attitudes, feelings, expectations and intentions?

— *Take in the whole picture:* People are not just cognitive in their orientations. They have feeling and values, which influence what they say and more importantly how they say it. Be attentive to the emotional tone and non-verbal cues, which are exhibited by a speaker while speaking.

— *Paraphrase:* Paraphrasing involves restating what the speaker has said in your own words and then checking to see whether the speaker agrees that you have caught the meaning of what was communicated. Effective ways of paraphrasing include using words such as: Do you mean that... What I hear you saying is...?

— *Integrate what is being said:* Use your spare time while listening to build a mental model of what the total viewpoint of the speaker is as it is evolving. Put the pieces together, rather than thinking of ways to tear them apart.

— *Avoid bias and distortion:* The purpose of active listening is to understand what the speaker is attempting to communicate to you. All people will use words or phrases in their discourse, which may be "red flags" to another person. Active listening requires that these words be temporarily placed in the background and not be used as code words to unfairly interpret, categorise or dismiss what the speaker is attempting to say.

Engaged Learning

In recent years, researchers have formed a strong consensus on the importance of engaged learning in schools and classrooms. This consensus, together with a recognition of the changing needs of the twenty-first century, has stimulated the development of specific indicators of engaged learning. Jones, Valdez, Nowakowski, and Rasmussen developed the indicators described below.

1. *Vision of Engaged Learning:* Successful, engaged learners are responsible for their own learning. These students are self-regulated and able to define their own learning goals and evaluate their own achievement. They are also energised by their learning; their joy of learning leads to a lifelong passion for solving problems, understanding, and taking the next step in their thinking. These learners are strategic in that they know how to learn and are able to transfer knowledge to solve problems creatively. Engaged learning also involves being collaborative, that is, valuing and having the skills to work with others.
2. *Tasks for engaged learning*: In order to have engaged learning, tasks need to be challenging, authentic, and multidisciplinary. Such tasks are typically complex and involve sust ined amounts of time. They are authentic in that they correspond to the tasks in the

home and workplaces of today and tomorrow. Collaboration around authentic tasks often takes place with peers and mentors within school as well as with family members and others in the real world outside of school. These tasks often require integrated instruction that incorporates problem-based learning and curriculum by project.

3. *Assessment of engaged learning:* Assessment of engaged learning involves presenting students with an authentic task, project, or investigation, and then observing, interviewing, and examining their presentations and artifacts to assess what they actually know and can do. This assessment, often called performance-based assessment, is generative in that it involves students in generating their own performance criteria and playing a key role in the overall design, evaluation, and reporting of their assessment. The best performance-based assessment has a seamless connection to curriculum and instruction so that it is ongoing. Assessment should represent all meaningful aspects of performance and should have equitable standards that apply to all students.

4. *Instructional models & strategies for engaged learning:* The most powerful models of instruction are interactive. Instruction actively engages the learner, and is generative. Instruction encourages the learner to construct and produce knowledge in meaningful ways. Students teach others interactively and interact generatively with their teacher and peers. This allows for co-construction of knowledge, which promotes engaged learning that is problem-, project-, and goal-based. Some common strategies included in engaged learning models of instruction are individual and group summarising, means of exploring multiple perspectives, techniques for building upon prior knowledge, brainstorming, Socratic dialogue, problem-solving processes, and team teaching.

5. *Learning context of engaged learning:* For engaged learning to happen, the classroom must be conceived of as a knowledge-building learning community. Such communities not only develop shared understandings collaboratively but also create empathetic learning environments that value diversity and multiple perspectives. These communities search for strategies to build on the strengths of all of its members. Truly collaborative classrooms, schools, and communities encourage students to ask hard questions, define problems, lead conversations, set goals, have work-related conversations with family members and other adults in and out of school, and engage in entrepreneurial activities.
6. *Grouping for engaged learning:* Collaborative work that is learning-centered often involves small groups or teams of two or more students within a classroom or across classroom boundaries. Heterogeneous groups (including different sexes, cultures, abilities, ages, and socioeconomic backgrounds) offer a wealth of background knowledge and perspectives to different tasks. Flexible grouping, which allows teachers to reconfigure small groups according to the purposes of instruction and incorporates frequent heterogeneous groups, is one of the most equitable means of grouping and ensuring increased learning opportunities.
7. *Teacher roles for engaged learning:* The role of the teacher in the classroom has shifted from the primary role of information giver to that of facilitator, guide, and learner. As a facilitator, the teacher provides the rich environments and learning experiences needed for collaborative study. The teacher also is required to act as a guide—a role that incorporates mediation, modelling, and coaching. Often the teacher also is a co-learner and co-investigator with the students.
8. *Student roles for engaged learning:* One important student role is that of explorer. Interaction with the physical world and with other people allows students to discover concepts and apply skills. Students are

then encouraged to reflect upon their discoveries, which is essential for the student as a cognitive apprentice. Apprenticeship takes place when students observe and apply the thinking processes used by practitioners. Students also become teachers themselves by integrating what they've learned. Hence, they become producers of knowledge, capable of making significant contributions to the world's knowledge.

Table 2: Indictors of Engaged Learning

Variable	*Indicator of Engaged Learning*	*Indicator Definition*
	Responsible for learning	Learner involved in setting goals, choosing tasks; has big picture of learning and next steps in mind.
Vision of Learning	Strategic	Learner actively develops repertoire of thinking/learning strategies.
	Energised by learning	Learner is not dependent on rewards from others; has a passion for learning.
	Collaborative	Learner develops new ideas and understanding in conversations and work with others.
	Authentic	Pertains to real world, may be addressed to personal interest.
Tasks	Challenging	Difficult enough to be interesting but not totally frustrating, usually sustained.

(Contd...)

(Contd...)

	Multidisciplinary	Involves integrating disciplines to solve problems and address issues.
	Performance-based	Involving a performance or demonstration, usually for a real audience and useful purpose.
	Generative	Assessments having meaning for learner; maybe produce information, product, service
Assessment	Seamless and ongoing	Assessment is part of instruction and vice versa; students learn during assessment
	Equitable	Assessment is culture fair
	Interactive	Teacher or technology programme responsive to student needs, requests (e.g., menu-driven)
Instructional Model	Generative	Instruction oriented to constructing meaning; providing meaningful activities/experiences
	Collaborative	Instruction conceptualises students as part of learning community; activities are collaborative
Learning Context	Knowledge-building	Learning experiences set up to bring multiple perspectives to solve problems such that each perspective contributes to shared understanding for all; goes beyond

(Contd...)

(Contd...)

		brainstorming
	Empathetic	Learning environment and experiences set up for valuing diversity, multiple perspectives, strengths.
Grouping	Heterogeneous	Small groups with persons from different ability levels and backgrounds
	Equitable	Small groups organised so that over time all students have challenging learning tasks/ experiences
	Flexible	Different groups organised for different instructional purposes so each person is a member of different groups; works with different people.
Teacher Roles	Facilitator	Engages in negotiation, stimulates and monitors discussion and project work but does not control
	Guide	Helps students to construct their own meaning by modelling, mediating, explaining when needed, redirecting focus, providing options
	Co-learner/co-investigator	Teacher considers self as learner; willing to take risks to explore areas outside his or her expertise;

(Contd...)

(Contd...)

		collaborates with other teachers and practicing professionals.
Student Roles	Explorer	Students have opportunities to explore new ideas/tools; push the envelope in ideas and research Cognitive apprentice learning is situated in relationship with mentor who coaches students to develop ideas and skills that simulate the role of practicing professionals (i.e., engage in real research)
	Teacher	Students encouraged to teach others in formal and informal contexts
	Producer	Students develop products of real use to themselves and others

These indicators of engaged learning can act as a "compass" for reform instruction, helping educators chart an instructional course and maintain an orientation based on a vision of engaged learning and what it looks like in the classroom and community.

Technology-enhanced programmes for engaged learning

There is strong consensus in the research community that technology and technology-enhanced programmes can promote engaged learning. There are many features of technology that are important to learning. Indicators for identifying effective, high technology performance, organised within six categories:

i) access that a school has to diverse technologies and resources, both within its own classrooms and beyond the school;

ii) operability of the technology;

iii) organisation of the technology in terms of its location and distribution;

iv) "engagability," or the capacity of the technology to engage students in challenging learning;

v) ease of use; and

vi) functionality, or the technology's capacity to prepare students to use a variety

vii) of technological tools.

Indicators of high performance that would promote engaged learning. Table 3 displays these indicators.

Table 3: Indicators of High Technology Performance

Variable	*Indicator of High Technology Performance*	*Indicator Definition*
	Connective	Schools are connected to internet and other resources.
Access	Ubiquitous	Technology resources and equipment are pervasive and conveniently located for individual (as opposed to centralised) use.
	Interconnective	Students and teachers interact by communicating and collaborating in diverse ways.
	Designed for equitable use	All students have access to rich,

(Contd...)

(Contd...)

		challenging learning opportunities and interactive, generative instruction.
	Interoperable	Capable of exchanging data easily among diverse formats and technologies.
Operability	Open architecture	Allows users to access third-party hardware/ software operates.
	Transparent	Users are not—and do not need to be—aware of how the hardware/software operates.
	Distributed	Technology/system resources are not centralised but exist across any number of people, environments and situations.
Organisation		
	Designed for user contributions	Users can provide input/resources to the technology/system on demand.
	Designed for colla-borative projects	Technology is designed to facilitate communication among users with diverse systems/ equipment.
	Access to chall-enging tasks	Technology offers or allows access to tasks, data, and learning opportunities that stimulate thought and inquiry.

(Contd...)

(Contd...)

Engagability	Enables learning by doing	Technology offers access to simulations, goals-based learning, and real-world problems.
	Provides guided participation	Technology responds intelligently to user and is able to diagnose and prescribe new learning.
	Effective helps	Technology provides help indices that are more than glossaries; may provide procedures for tasks and routines.
Ease of Use	User friendliness/ user control	Technology facilitates user and is free from overly complex procedures; user can easily access data and tools on demand.
	Fast	Technology has a fast processing speed and is not "down" for long periods of time.
	Available training and support	Training is readily and conveniently available, as is ongoing support.
	Provides just enough information just in time	Technology allows for random access, multiple points of entry, and different levels and types of information.
	Diverse tools	Technology enables access to full diversity of generic and context—specified

(Contd...)

(Contd...)

		tools basic to learning and working in the 21st century.
	Media use	Technology provides opportunities to use media technologies.
Functionality	Promotes programming and authoring	Technology provides tools (e.g.,"wizards") that are used to make other tools.
	Supports project design skills	Technology facilitates the development of skills related to project design and implementation.

Issues in engaged learning

In order for technology to effectively promote engaged learning for all students, certain elements inside and outside the classroom must be in place. Technology is a tool that gives everyone an equal chance to learn. Given its significance in national and local policy, the first issue concerns equity, or the goal of universal participation. Policy makers at a national level have made a commitment to building a national infrastructure and achieving universal participation. But that's not enough. State policy makers must make this commitment as well, since the bulk of technology funding is expected to come from states.

Universal participation, as a policy goal, means that all students in all schools have access to and are active on the information highway in ways that support engaged learning. Inequities will be reduced because everyone will have equal access and equal opportunity to learn. However, the danger is that many poor schools will be precluded from these learning activities because:

i) schools don't have the funds to buy the needed technology;

ii) curricula and assessment programmes focus on low-level skills even when technology is applied;

iii) teachers don't have the support they need to develop instructional strategies to use with the information they can access through the technology; and

iv) bureaucracies keep communication and development from moving beyond the walls of the school into business and community sectors.

Today's educational system centralises the purchase and distribution of textbooks, equipment, supplies, and services. Such a top-down approach permits cost-effective, high-volume purchasing. But, it is also terribly out of step with today's needs. The new technology-driven organisation must address this issue. Technology legislation in progress may alleviate some of the funding crisis and go some distance toward helping poor schools provide ongoing professional development. Nevertheless, it is quite possible that richer schools—which are able to access and use information and research resources—will get "information richer," while poor schools, by comparison, will become significantly "information poorer".

Employability is an important concern for all students, and experience with a technology that has high transferability to the community and workplace is crucial. Coordination involves many different policy players and many different configurations of technology and telecommunications. Private and public sector planning could facilitate shared financing and improve technology access and use in school-to-work programmes.

Some school-to-work transition initiatives promote students' use of workplace technologies. For example, museum exhibits and specially designed workstations in schools give students sustained learning experiences with high-performance technologies that promote engaged learning. Two emerging models of teaching and learning address the focus on school-to-work transition: cognitive apprenticeships and knowledge-building communities. These models emerge from research on learning, but have a natural affinity for school-to-work issues because both seek to engage learners and communities in the social relationships so critical in the workplace.

Electronic networks will enable schools to receive up-to-the-minute data from every sector of society around the globe. Schools will become part of a worldwide network with research agencies and practising professionals to build knowledge communities. Many of the new data sets they access will be in picture and video formats. Therefore, video networking, integration, and management in schools will become critical. A major part of this infrastructure is the development of digital libraries and museum learning environments to help students and teachers access, browse, manipulate, and interact with image and video data.

The internet and emerging video and imaging technologies could change not only how schools get information and services, but also the very economics of school service delivery itself. The content and services available through the internet and other telecommunications resources could ultimately replace most of the textbooks and other costly instructional materials, software, and programmes that currently bite hard into most school budgets. If schools were to draw largely upon these free resources and services, they could spend far more of their budgets on staffing, curriculum development, technology growth, staff development, and school restructuring.

The widespread application of technology to promote engaged learning will yield several exciting changes in the ways schools organise curricula, define teacher and student roles, and structure themselves. These changes, in turn, will significantly effect student achievement.

Problem-based Learning

One essential goal of education is the development of students who are effective problem solvers for the Information Literacy Age. Most school goal statements allude to the need for critical thinking and problem solving skills. But often such instruction in problem solving takes the approach of teaching models to students to apply to neat case studies rather than the messy problems of a real world.

Research indicates that critical thinking and problem solving skills are not typically addressed in the classroom. A number of studies indicate that in the typical classroom, 85 per cent of teacher questions are at the recall or simple comprehension level. Questions that elicit synthesis and evaluative skills of thinking are rarely asked.

In Problem-based learning (PBL) environments, students act as professionals and confront problems as they occur—with fuzzy edges, insufficient information, and a need to determine the best solution possible by a given date. This is the manner in which engineers, doctors, and, yes, even teachers, approach problem solving, unlike many classrooms where teachers are the "sage on the stage" and guide students to neat solutions to contrived problems.

Problem-based learning is a curriculum development and delivery system that recognises the need to develop problem solving skills as well as the necessity of helping students to acquire necessary knowledge and skills. Indeed, the first application of PBL was in medical schools which rigorously test the knowledge base of graduates. PBL utilises real world problems, not hypothetical case studies with neat, convergent outcomes. It is in the process of struggling with actual problems that students learn both content and critical thinking skills.

Problem based learning thus has several distinct characteristics which may be identified and utilised in designing such curriculum. These are:

— Reliance on problems to drive the curriculum—the problems do not test skills; they assist in development of the skills themselves.

— The problems are truly ill-structured—there is not meant to be one solution, and as new information is gathered in a reiterative process, perception of the problem, and thus the solution, changes.

— Students solve the problems — teachers are coaches and facilitators.

— Students are only given guidelines for how to approach problems — there is no one formula for student approaches to the problem.
— Authentic, performance-based assessment — is a seamless part and end of the instruction.

Problem-based learning assists students to solve problems by the process of continually encountering the type of ill-structured problems confronted by adults or practicing professionals. As with information literacy, PBL develops students who can:

— Clearly define a problem.
— Develop alternative hypotheses.
— Access, evaluate, and utilise data from a variety of sources.
— Alter hypotheses given new information.
— Develop clearly stated solutions that fit the problem and its inherent conditions, based upon information and clearly explicated reasoning.

Students with such ingrained skill are well prepared for occupations which rarely have a supervisor who has time, inclination, or knowledge to tell the worker what to do. They are also well prepared for the explosion of knowledge which gluts the world today.

Stages in problem-based learning

In the PBL curriculum, one may note three distinct phases of operation by students. Whether gathering knowledge through a variety of sources on the internet, through print sources, or by speaking with experts, these stages explicated below are characteristic of PBL. Each step in the process is "hot linked" to a sample lesson developed by a SCORE Teacher on Assignment.

Stage 1: *Encountering and defining the problem:* Students are confronted with a real world scenario through authentic looking correspondence. Students may be asked to present to the Ancient World Architectural Review Board regarding their perspective about how and why great ancient monuments were built. They may ask some basic questions such as :

What do I know already about this problem or question?

What do I need to know to effectively address this problem or question?

What resources can I access to determine a proposed solution or hypothesis?

At this point, a very focused problem statement is needed, though that statement will be altered as new information is accessed and understood.

Stage 2: *Accessing, evaluating and utilising information:* Once they have clearly defined the problem, students might access print, human, or electronic information resources. In the case of the Southern Illinois Medical School, professors may be interviewed or medical texts examined. In the case of a city plan, calls to human resources such as the town manager or staff engineers might be of use. The internet can be a focal point of research when a problem is constructed with that purpose. In the case of the sample problem, students may find a rich diversity of perspectives and resources preparatory to phase 3. Part of any problem is evaluation of the resource. How current is it? How credible and accurate is it? Is there any reason to suspect bias in the source? When utilising the information, students must carefully appraise the worth of the sources they have accessed. If evaluating sites which theorise about these monuments and how and why they were built, students must carefully note and evaluate the accuracy and credibility of information posted at that site.

Stage 3: *Synthesis and performance:* In this stage, students construct a solution to the problem. Students may create a multi-media production, a presentation to a body such as the UN Commission on Human Rights or the Ancient World Architectural Review Board, or a more traditional written paper focused around an essential question. In all cases, the students must re-organise the information is new ways. This is unlike an assignment which asks them to "make a report about the Palestinians and Israelis." This latter leads to use of the internet as if it were a giant cyberspace encyclopedia. An assignment which asks students to propose a solution to the conflict between the Palestinian people and the Israelis involves a question which forces re-organisation of information and consideration of perspectives.

Implementation of PBL

Cultural change is required to implement PBL. Students trained in the more traditional model of teaching, which features the teacher as "sage on the stage" and disseminator of knowledge, will experience culture shock of a sort. Students will wish to know expectations for a high grade. Though constructing a rubric with a teacher may allay fears, there is initial suspicion of the new approach. Students must also learn to be part of the group. As with real life tasks, one person cannot conduct all research and make the entire presentation of the problem solution. Complaints about "hitchhikers" (those in the group who do not pull their own weight) will be heard from hard working students and their parents.

Teachers also experience major adjustments. More preliminary work must be done to design the problem and to ensure that there are enough materials available (in print, online, and through human resources) for this resource's ravenous approach. They must learn to construct problems that assist students to learn appropriate skills and knowledge. And they must learn to facilitate, rather than direct, student learning.

Though change from a teacher-centred to a problem and project-based environment causes discomfort, those that have made the transition speak of new energy and enthusiasm for their classes. Students praise challenging tasks that prepare them for learning.

Whole-language Approach

Educators have long agreed that real reading includes thoughts, but they have long argued about what is the best way to teach real reading. Some more traditionalists use a phonetic approach, where children learn the sounds of certain letters, and when they see those letters in combination, they learn to blend those letters, and this forms a word. As they become comfortable forming that word, they learn to think about its meaning, and so decoding leads to thought, or real reading.

Many reading programmes are primarily based on a phonetic approach to the teaching of reading. In the early grades, children learn that certain letters make certain familiar sounds which they repeat in unison and separately until they can almost do it in their sleep! Then if you were to visit a classroom you would see how even the toughest of words can be "sounded" out, discussed on context, and children's working vocabularies grow. Almost any words can be sounded out—even ones that are not spelled phonetically when exceptions to the rule are learned. This is the traditional approach to learning to read and proponents of this system argue that children are most successful by using this approach.

Yet in recent years, another approach, namely, "whole language" approach, has become increasingly popular. According to the whole language or meaning approach, children can learn to recognise several words as easily as they can some letters, so rather than feed the words to them letter by letter, the teacher should provide for them a complete word so they can focus immediately on meaning. So whole language people would organise the grade one classroom differently. They would teach 50-75 words by sight method, with someone telling the child each word. They would use a story method approach with a very short story read to children, picking out key words, putting them on an experience chart and examining new words in relation to memorised ones. When phonics is necessary, it would by analysis rather than by synthesis. Practically, this means that whole language people say that children learn to read much as they learn to speak. Instead of children being presented with a list of words to decipher phonetically, (after some initial phonics) they would be presented for example with a story. After discussing the story, they may agree that some key words were bike, boy, store, man and ball. These words would then be placed on the board and studied for their spelling, etc. Words and language are not taken from an artificial list, but from the children's reading experience. And there is also a lot of emphasis on writing. Communication is more important in whole language than correctness, ideas more important than precision.

Whole language means that you immerse the child with reading and with writing, and, just as he learns to speak, he will "pick up" the words that are relevant for him to read. And as he grows and matures, his vocabulary necessarily increases as his world expands.

Proponents of phonetics are severely critical of this method, Some even hold it responsible for the growing illiteracy in our country. They are appalled at the seeming acceptance of inaccuracy in order to achieve comfort and self-confidence. Furthermore, they claim that whole language is humanistic. They claim it is based on the principle that a child does not need rules and structure in order to learn, that given the right environment, learning will just come naturally.

Defendants of whole language cry treason. Phonics they say emphasises academics, empty-intellectual- academics, at the expense of a pupil's emotional and social development. Phonics people march staunchly onward, hog-washing the humanistic trends of emotional and social concerns. Perhaps a programme which is primarily phonics-oriented is best. However, the teachers in the classrooms should not be exclusively phonics-oriented. A phonetic approach can be used to word study, but it should be amply supplemented with stories, experience charts, sight words, word comparisons, writing and writing skills, etc., to make language relevant.

Future Challenges of Learning

The learning plays in sustainable development and its contribution in particular to poverty reduction and income generation, empowerment and consolidation of democracy, disease prevention and sustainable health and to the protection of the environment is by now well known. Education, learning and acquisition of knowledge and skills have never been more central than they are today.

We are living in an age of unprecedented change. Technological, cultural and social upheavals have impacted upon us with regularity and increasing ferocity, radically changing the way we live, work and learn. Accelerating change has often overtaken even the most stable of our social institutions, including education, and the rate of change will no doubt increase with gathering speed in the years ahead. Various dimensions of the change are illustrated in figure 1.

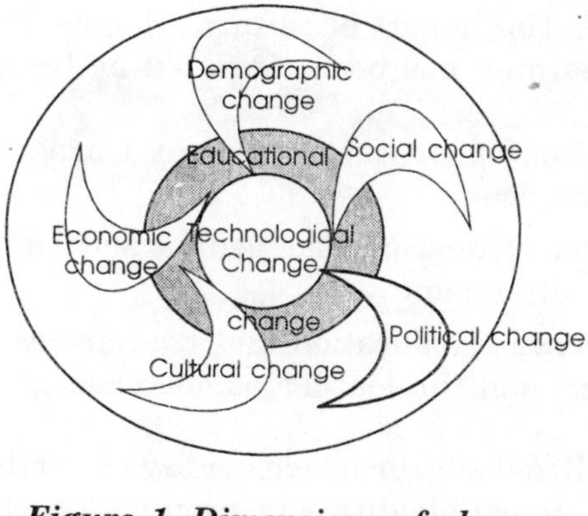

Figure 1. Dimensions of change

This dimensions of change, while distinct, are also closely interrelated. Together, they will shape the ways in which people will address the learning challenges of the future. It is widely acknowledged that the following features of change have a profound impact on the future of learning:

i) nature of change;
ii) nature of response to change;
iii) speed of change;
iv) conceptualisation of change; and
v) changes in identities to individuals and groups.

The change is one of the most crucial aspects. Accelerating rates of change apply immense pressure on individuals for skilling, re-skilling and multi-skilling in response to changing demands for "work skills" and "life skills". The requirements for flexibility and competitiveness are a necessary corollary to economic change in the increasingly "insecure" world of work. The types and organisation of the workplace and of skills needed by workers and employers are in a constant state of flux. In order to cope with these changes, it has become essential to build flexible, multi-skilled workers.

In the case of cultural change, three dimensions have been recognised. They include individualisation, lifestyle and consumption. The impact of cultural change on development of lifelong learning has been mediated by three features:

i) promotion of informed choice by learners in an age of consumerism;
ii) creation of new market genres such as infotainment and edutainment; and
iii) emergence of education and training as products and services and the learner as customer or client.

Changing lifestyle practices play a critical role in construction of self-identity and adoption of learning modes. The culture of consumption is also supported by a growing private sector of providers of educational opportunities. Changes in the demographic profile of populations can have a substantial influence on the nature and scope for lifelong learning. The ageing of the population and addition of older adults no longer active in the labour market would pose particular challenges in the provision of opportunities for lifelong learning.

In developing countries, young people account for a large population share. This creates its own demands for learning opportunities. The type of learning opportunities provided, the nature of learning providers and specific inputs for enabling people to use information and communication technologies are critical issues. Technological change is a major determinant of economic, cultural and demographic changes. Technological change, for example, conditions the existence and nature of employment. It lays frameworks for competitiveness, new forms of employment and ways of organising work.

Technological change, especially emergence of new information and communication technologies, has had a profound impact on culture. It has governed the instant impact of events; compressed time and space; fuelled consumerism; created new computer and satellite mediated forms of social interaction and pushed up the demand for learning the use of the new media and technological tools.

The dual role of technological change in relation to lifelong learning deserves careful scrutiny. First, technological change creates conditions for lifelong learning. Second, technological change opens up new possibilities for designing, producing and delivering learning inputs and therefore helps to support lifelong learning. The new technologies have served to push knowledge acquisition into the domain of the individual.

Technology, and particularly its application in flexible, open and distance learning situations can be considered vital for increasing and widening access to learning and for the learner to become more autonomous. Flexibility of open and distance learning methodologies is the key factor in their emergence as the primary mode for lifelong learning. Also, learning to learn using new technologies or, in other words, building techno-literacy can help to build the confidence to use the technology as a tool to further the learning experience even without the mediation of a learning institution.

Science and technology will be the primary forces of change in every aspect of society. The world will experience more quantum leaps in information and communication technology. The integration—or fusion—of continuing revolution in information technology, biotechnology, material science, and nanatechnology will generate enormous opportunity to create new knowledge, its storage and its intelligent utilisation for the well-being of humanity. But, it could also widen the gap between the rich and the poor unless effective measures are taken to harness the potential of science of technology to help the poor.

The networked and interdependent global economy will be driven by rapid and largely unrestricted flows of information, ideas, cultural values, capital, goods and services, and people: that is globalisation. The developing countries can benefit from globalisation only, if they can provide opportunities for their people to acquire knowledge, skills and attitudes to be competitive globally.

Developing countries will face both, internal conflicts and regional interstate wars stemming from religious, ethnic, economic or political disputes. The number of refugees, homeless or displaced people may increase significantly requiring educational provision of a very different kind. The globalising economy and technological change inevitably place increasing premium on a more highly skilled labour force. However, the progress in education will vary among regions, countries and societal groups, triggering further inequalities within as well as among countries.

Some argue that the income gap between the rich and the poor is increasing nationally and internationally. But while income is perhaps the most visible manifestation of inequality, and income poverty the most visible form of deprivation, the less visible disparities in education are reinforcing both inequality and poverty. The poorest countries and poorest people are those with the least access to educational opportunity. In future, the linkages between education and other forms of deprivation will be further strengthened by globalisation, technological change, and the communication revolution. There are a number of other major barriers to learning opportunities. These are:

i) increasing access;
ii) reaching the disadvantaged groups and communities;
iii) providing educational inputs of good quality;
iv) making educational opportunities available at affordable cost;
v) enhancing the relevance of educational provision to societal and individual needs; and
vi) providing opportunities for lifelong learning.

Inequality in access to education is seen at different levels: between north and south; between developing countries and within countries. Inequality in access to education within countries takes many forms: differences between men and women, urban and rural areas, and ethnic groups. In developing countries, men living in rural areas are twice as likely to be illiterate as those living in urban areas. A number of factors are responsible for such disparities such as:

i) administration cost,
ii) unwillingness of teacher to live in remote rural areas,
iii) public spending priorities and demands for child labour.

Transition in Open and Distance Learning

The World Education Forum emphasised that "Education is a fundamental human right. It is key to sustainable development and peace and stability within and among countries, and thus an indispensable means for effective participation in the societies and economies of the twenty-first century. Achieving EFA goals should be postponed no longer. The basic learning needs of all can be and must be met as a matter of urgency."

The age-old methods of educational delivery cannot adequately meet the growing demand for learning has led to several innovations—open learning, distance education, flexible learning, distributed learning and more recently online education, e-learning or virtual education. These innovations have brought about many changes in:

i) learner profile and the role of learner;
ii) role of teacher;
iii) venue of learning;
iv) nature of content and content development process;
v) learner support system;
vi) method of educational delivery;
vii) organisational structure;
viii) financing of education;
ix) assessment of learning outcome; and
x) certification.

In recent years, the use of open and distance learning methodologies has been growing rapidly both in developed and developing countries. The advances in communication and information technologies is the single most important factor in the growth of open and distance learning in recent years, and it will continue to play a significant role in the future growth as well. ICTs bridge the geographical and transactional distance between the teachers and the learners and provide unique opportunities to meet the rapidly increasing demand for learning throughout the life in the resource-scarce environments.

The ICTs help overcome geographical, economic and socio-cultural barriers; provide greater interactivity; reduce cost; enhance virtual proximity and access; bring greater variety of learning resources and provide greater flexibility and learner control. The technical capacity of ICTs has far exceeded the capacity of the educational community to respond fully to the opportunities and challenges this rapid change has brought. Despite the demonstrated potential of ICTs in open and distance learning, most developing countries experience several constraints in exploiting the potential of ICTs fully. These are:

i) access to technologies;
ii) cost of technologies;
iii) lack of infrastructure;
iv) lack of adequately trained human resources;
v) language barriers;
vi) institutional barriers;
vii) lack of techno-literacy; and
viii) policy and regulatory constraints.

ICTs offer the best hope to provide learning opportunities to the disadvantaged individual and groups. There are some of the strategies that could be used to remove barriers to learning:

Multiple media approach: The learners are best served where a whole battery of media, old and new, are used. This is because one medium may serve a teaching function better than another in a particular area, and learners may have different preferences for the media they best learn from. Differences in the cognitive styles of individuals have long been recognised in the field of educational communication. The socio-economic and cultural background of a person also influences his ability to learn from different media.

Emphasis on appropriate technologies: Distance education programmes and institutions vary in their size of student population, number and level of courses offered, financial and physical resources, capability of the staff to use technologies, availability of physical infrastructure and a host of other variables. Finding an appropriate media mix is one of the major tasks of distance education providers. But there is no scientific procedure for deciding the "best" media configuration. Planners of distance education systems have to custom design their media mix to suit the circumstances in which they operate.

Integration of technology and training: There is considerable evidence from the world over that to ensure effective utilisation of technologies for education, training must be an integral part of overall planning and implementation. Effective utilisation of technology requires a proper understanding of the potential, and the strengths and weaknesses of different technologies at all levels-planners and administrators, academics, instructional designers, and those responsible for developing and producing educational material for delivery. Attention must also be paid to developing the technical skills to ensure that the full potential of technology is realised. Training in instructional design for using different technology is equally if not more important.

Unlike conventional teaching, distance education involves teamwork between academics, instructional designers and media producers and a host of other technical staff. Training plays a vital role in developing proper understanding of each other's role and in building a team approach. Training the distance learner in the effective use of technology for learning is yet another important area of training. Training, therefore, must be regarded as an integral part of planning for the use of technology.

Sustainability: The capital cost of acquiring technology is not the only cost incurred in using technology. The recurring cost of producing educational material must be an important consideration. Unless there is strong justification to use professional grade television or video, other options such as low-cost video or audio may be more cost effective. This consideration is often ignored when donor agencies meet the capital cost of the hardware.

User friendliness, compatibility with the existing technologies, availability of spare parts and maintenance services, and adaptability to emerging technologies are some of the other factors that need to be taken into consideration in selecting technologies. While these factors are important, in practice, media selection and use is determined by a number of macro-level and micro-level factors. Some of the most important macro-level factors are: country size (area and population), wealth and resources, extent of industriali-sation, education and training system infrastructure and capabilities, political support for education and educational technology, and information dissemination infrastructure. These factors can suggest the kinds of technology that best fit a country's economic and socio-political circumstances.

Community access approach: Countries such as India are making steady progress in internet use. There are over 2.5 million internet users in India. This figure is likely to grow twenty eight fold in the next eight years to 70 million. The information technology industry is expected to record a phenomenal 40 per cent growth rate for the next three years. In recent years community telecentres have emerged as a feasible alternative in reaching people who have remained isolated from the information revolution and at the periphery of development. The use of community information and communication centres have been recommended as possible support structures for open learning and creation of the connected learning community.

References

Barrows, H., *Practice-Based Learning: Problem-Based Learning Applied to Medical Education*, Springfield, Il: Southern Illinois University School of Medicine, 1994.

Boud, D., Felleti, G., *The Challenge of Problem-Based Learning*, London: Kogan, 1991.

Dalton, D. W., "The effect of cooperative learning strategies on achievement and attitudes during interactive video", *Journal of Computer-Based Instruction*, 1990.

Gagne, R. M. and Briggs L., *Principles of Instructional Design*. Holt, Rinehart and Winston, New York, 1979.

Gagne, R., L. Briggs, & W. Wager, *Principles of instructional Design* (4th Ed.) , Fort Worth, TX: HBJ College, 1992.

Gibbons, A. S., & P. G., Fairweather, *Computer-based instruction: design and development*, Englewood Cliffs, NJ: Educational Technology Publications, 1998.

Jones, B., Valdez, G., Nowakowski, J., & Rasmussen, C., *Designing Learning and Technology for Educational Reform*, Oak Brook, IL: North Central Regional Educational Laboratory, 1994.

Reigeluth, C. M., "Instructional design: What is it and why is it?", In C. M. Reigeluth (Ed.), *Instructional design theories and models: An overview of their current status*, Hillsdale, NJ: Lawrence Erlbaum Associates, 1983.

Rheingold, H., *Virtual Community: Homesteading on the Electronic Frontier*, Cambridge MA:MIT Press, 2000.

Rogoff, B., *Apprenticeship in thinking: Cognitive development in social context*, New York: Oxford University Press, 1990.

Schank, R. C., Berman, T. R., Macpherson, K. A., "Learning by doing", In C. M. Reigeluth (Ed.), *Instructional-design theories and models*, Volume II, 1999.

South, J. B., Monson, D. W., "A university-wide system for creating, capturing, and delivering learning objects", In D. Wiley Ed., *The instructional use of learning objects*, Bloomington IN: Association for Educational Communications and Technology, 2002.

Stepien, W.J. and Gallagher, S.A., "Problem-based Learning: As Authentic as it Gets", *Educational Leadership*. 50(7) 25-8, 1993.

Woods, Donald R., *Problem-Based Learning: How to Gain the Most from PBL*, Hamilton, Ontario, Canada, Donald R. Woods, Publisher, 1994.

3

Multicultural Understanding in Teaching and Learning

Multicultural education is a field which itself mirrors the level of cultural fragmentation evident in society. It is education that focuses on providing equal opportunity for students whose cultural and/or language patterns make it difficulty for them to succeed in traditional school programmes. Many multicultural programmes also emphasise positive intergroup and interracial attitudes and contacts. However, it should not be inferred that (multiculturalism) is intended only to bolster the self-image and enhance the learning of minority students.

Francesina Jackson describes a multicultural approach to education founded upon the following criteria: building trust, becoming culturally literate, building a repertoire of instructional strategies, using effective questioning techniques, providing effective feedback, analysing instructional materials, and establishing positive home-school relations.

Multicultural education is by no means a universally accepted approach. While space prohibits an exhaustive presentation of its critics, one asserts that multicultural education has been overshadowed by bitter debate, which has heightened racial and ethnic tension. An essential idea in most multicultural approaches to education is the inherent worth and dignity of the represented culture and the individuals who comprise them.

A worldview is defined as "A set of values, assumptions and core beliefs that individuals use to interpret the world around them: the lens that the individuals use to describe and explains issues, events and conditions." Taken from the field of international relations, worldview theory essentially states that if there are five billion people on the planet, then there are five billion worldviews.

The teacher is in the classroom to provide a learning environment for the students, not to play the role of therapist or psychologist. The teacher to utilise instructional methodology and design teaching techniques and activities to engage the multicultural nature of the class as an asset. It also alerts the teacher about how to assist individual students who may be having particular challenges adjusting to a new environment and life. Teachers should also know where and how to refer students appropriately, should the teacher notice a behaviour that may represent a student's need for mental health intervention.

What are some of the instructional strategies teachers might call upon specifically to address the challenges presented by the multicultural classroom? Many of these activities probably have been used in many different class settings. However, thinking about them with an eye to enhancing opportunities for learning based on multicultural experiences and needs may mean the teacher manages both the content and the details of presentation and participation differently.

Children need to experience the classroom as a safe environment where they can tell their stories or be encouraged to draw or write. Journals often are a good way for this to happen because they provide privacy. However even in journals, students should never feel pressure to reveal more than they are willing or want to declare. Assignments should be broad enough so that every child can participate without feeling discomfort about the subject or the memories and experiences it brings up for them. On the other hand, such assignments may give students opportunities to work through difficult facets of their life by simply being listened to.

Although the multicultural classroom contains a cacophony of differences, there are likely more similarities present between the students than differences. These can be building blocks to help children from various cultures learn to relate to each other and to the world at large. Having students work in pairs and small groups also gives them opportunities to share and risk and to get to know each other more than some might in a large group setting. This also provides opportunities to handle both the usual multilevel and multicultural aspects of the classroom.

The multicultural classroom may at first be uncomfortable and challenging to both teachers and students. However, managed well, it can provide the richest of environments for learning, both to students and teachers. It can be a major factor in helping students adjust to a new culture, and be successful in school.

Every classroom is a cultural community reflective of the disciplines and perspectives studied, the authors, the students, and the professor. One can argue that successful learning requires an intercultural approach where students are responsible for listening (and reading and experiencing) to understand—both the perspectives of others (peers, authors, faculty) and for understanding their own perspectives and how they acquired them.

Students can come to understand that learning is about the generation, mutual reflection, and critiquing and expanding of ideas and concepts, and that this is most effectively done in a collaborative and non-competitive environment. One effective approach to this challenge is to attend to the variety of learning styles in any college classroom. Understanding multiple learning styles allows one to focus on individual students' own learning styles; subgroups within a classroom community; and the class as a learning community. Even in the most transformed classes, however, faculty are often unaware of the variety of pedagogies that can produce enhanced learning for students and faculty and that can facilitate growth in intellectual complexity and capacity.

Teachers can make students explicitly aware of how they and others learn; they can discuss strengths and weaknesses in various learning methods. Teachers can help students develop capacities in all *four* learning styles regardless of individual preferences for some styles over others. Student can also learn that there are patterns of values, speech, preferences, and behaviours associated with different cultures, and they can learn that there are as many differences within cultural groups as there are across different cultures. This helps students break down cultural stereotypes in the society as a whole.

Using these methods, students learn that they each may have a unique learning pattern and this realisation of their own "multiple subjectivities" can help them understand the multiple and interlocking identities in the people and groups around them. The classroom then becomes a living laboratory for negotiating individual and group differences as well as for negotiating ideas about the content and concepts of the class.

Multicultural education through Internet

The world wide web, which houses virtual libraries, museums, dialogue forums, reference collections, research databases, and historical archives from around the world, offers a collection of new educational opportunities for educators and students. The web has the potential to transcend the capabilities of many other multicultural media in its supplemental value to multicultural teaching practices. The key for unlocking this potential lies in understanding and using the web not merely as an enormous compendium of informational resources, but more importantly as an interactive medium that can connect people across borders and boundaries. With this in mind, there are clear intersections between some of the important ideals in multicultural curriculum transformation and the educational opportunities presented by the web. Those intersections are interactive, inclusive, and collaborative teaching and learning.

Interactive Teaching and Learning

The interactive opportunities made possible by the web can transcend the potential of most other educational media as a means to connect students with first person sources beyond classroom walls and national borders and across cultures. Most website creators provide an email address and/or other contact information so that teachers, students, and others can, in fact, contact them with questions, challenges, critiques, or comments.

The conceptualisation of interactive media not only refers to interacting with software or the web structure itself, but to interacting with people. It is the ability to facilitate interaction among people – interactive teaching and learning –that provides the foundation for the other two intersections of multicultural education and the web: inclusive and collaborative teaching and learning.

Inclusive Teaching and Learning

Many educators understand inclusive teaching as incorporating diverse voices and perspectives in the classroom. To them, inclusion is about finding materials and tools that are representative of the students in the classroom. Multicultural education takes this concept a step further. If education is truly to be student-centred, then the experiences, perspectives, and ideas of the students themselves must be brought to the fore in the educational experience. To be "included" in the educational process, students, as well as teachers, must be given opportunities to have their voices heard and to hear each others' voices.

The web is helping to facilitate this kind of inclusivity through countless sites that encourage teachers and students to participate in virtual global communities with other teachers and students who may be either very culturally similar or different. Sites such as KIDLINK and Cyber-Kids Interactive were created to facilitate peer learning experiences for students who want to share their ideas, poetry, art, and perspectives with other students around the world.

Collaborative Teaching and Learning

Collaborative and interdisciplinary teaching and learning are concepts that have been introduced, attempted, and reintroduced for decades. It is not uncommon for a group of teachers from a particular school to combine efforts in an attempt to connect lessons from subject to subject. In fact, for many teachers who struggle with time constraints and burn-out, sharing resources and collaborative planning become vital aspects of day-to-day classroom operations. For others, it is an avenue for modeling constructive and cooperative bridge-building across groups.

As with interactive and inclusive teaching and learning, the web has the potential to greatly expand the breadth and depth of collaborative possibilities of educators. The web helps to share resources and engage in collaborative planning and curriculum transformation processes around the world. Several websites help facilitate this exchange of ideas and resources. Nicknacks Telecollaborate Site and PedagoNet are virtual global collaborative sites where educators can share lesson plans and curriculum transformation projects that have worked well for them and others can download or print these resources for their own use. Some similar sites include complementary discussion forums, allowing users to more deeply discuss their teaching successes and failures and how the resources on the site can contribute to positive educational experiences for students and teachers.

Intercultural Networking

The internet can facilitate cross-cultural communication, interpersonal bridge-building, and intercultural networking. It can expand one's resource base virtually infinitely and diversify it to a previously unthinkable extent. Below are some strategies for using the internet to do just that – expand one's resource base by networking across cultures, national boundaries, and even comfort zones.

Web-based dialogue forums

Web-based dialogue forums come in two forms: discussion boards (or bulletin boards) and chat rooms. In both cases, these forums allow people to use the web to engage in dialogue about a variety of topics with others interested in those topics from around the world. Beyond the exchange of ideas and experiences, these forums allow you to connect with other people with similar interests and passions, forming networks that can become support groups, not only for teaching projects, but also for collectively engaging in the process of continually challenging ourselves to expand our understandings of both self and society. Several discussion boards and chat rooms currently exist that deal specifically with multicultural education and related issues.

Email discussion forums

Several email discussion forums (listservs or mailing lists) exist that deal specifically with multicultural education and related issues. Participants can post messages to a list address, and those messages are then circulated to the rest of the forum's subscribers via email. Like discussion boards, email forums provide participants with the opportunity to network with other people interested in a particular topic and to engage in challenging and thought-provoking dialogue on a variety of issues.

Email forums tend to be more intimate and personal than discussion boards. Since people generally participate in email forums over a considerable length of time, the names and email addresses flashing into everyone's mailbox can become familiar. This can provide an opportunity to make more personal connections with other educators or activists from around the world.

Educational Web Resources

The primary reason teachers give for not incorporating computer technology into classroom practice is a lack of training or knowledge about how to use products such as CD-ROMs and websites. Educators, already pressured by time constraints, are often intimidated by a perceived learning curve when it comes to developing better computer skills. For many, this feeling is exacerbated when they finally learn enough about the web to navigate around cyberspace and do simple searches, and suddenly find themselves lost in a maze of broken links, pornographic sites, and educational sites that have little or no original content or that have not been updated since 1996.

For every content-rich, credible educational website, there are literally hundreds, if not thousands, of sites that fit into one of several other categories including:

i) sites designed for commercial purposes, to sell a service or product;
ii) sites that are primarily composed of links to other sites with little or no original content or resources;
iii) sites with unidentified or unqualified content contributors;
iv) sites that no longer exist or have been moved to a new, unknown server; and
v) sites that have been abandoned or not updated for several years.

The abundance of sites that fall into these categories can make the process of finding useful and credible multicultural teaching and learning resources in the cyber-world a formidable challenge.

Several media and educational organisations are familiar for producing TV shows, films, CD-ROMs, books, and other teaching and learning materials that support multicultural ideals and curriculum development. The National Geographic Society, the Discovery Channel, the Public Broadcasting Company (PBS) and others have been part of the classrooms of developed countries for years. Like other educational organisations and companies, National Geographic, PBS, and others recognise that in order to remain competitive in today's market, they need to include a strong and visible web presence among their multiple projects. As a result, they have developed a series of techniques and strategies for attracting web users to their sites. One strategy many organisations employ to bring users to their sites is to provide free educational materials and resources. In fact, there seems to be a competition brewing among those companies known for producing educational media to offer more, and better, resources than their competitors.

Teachers and students are among the winners of this competition, reaping the benefits of several sites scrambling to outdo their competitors. Companies that are already known for producing quality educational materials have a vested interest in offering only wellresearched and well-evaluated resources. So one simple strategy for digging through the dirt to find quality classroom resources on the web quickly is to turn directly to the websites of National Geographic Society, the Discovery Channel, and others who have a reputation for producing effective educational media and whose products have been proven effective in your classroom.

In many cases, these sites offer entire sections such as 'Teaching Tools' or 'Lesson Plans' or 'Student Resources'. Many actually host online learning activities for students and discussion forums for educators. Some allow you to download a variety of educational materials including maps, audio and video clips, worksheets, and historical documents. Companies who have built reputations by producing and supporting quality educational projects and resources know that it is in their best interest to provide only high quality resources through the web.

Most of the criteria used to assess and evaluate traditional educational media such as textbooks and films can be directly applied to websites as well. These include: accuracy of the information, critical analysis of possible bias, credibility of the author and/or publishing source, appropriateness and accessibility to the specified audience, timeliness, relevance to a particular subject area, validity of content, and effectiveness of aesthetic aspects.

For a variety reasons, even deeper considerations for some of the more traditional educational evaluation criteria and several new criteria must be added to old models to holistically evaluate products of this fairly new cyber-medium. For instance, unlike traditional educational media such as films, textbooks, and journals that usually go through a rigorous review process before being made widely available to teachers and students, virtually anybody with access to a web server can create an educational website. In most cases, there is no entity comparable to a publishing company to help ensure the credibility or expertise of educational web designers. Likewise, as is the case with many journals, there is no formal review board to examine the validity of the information on most educational websites. For the most part, the responsibility is left with the user to assess these issues.

Other complications to the assessment of websites exist within the structure of the medium itself. In no other medium is the line between commercial and informational distinctions quite so blurry. Sometimes it is difficult to ascertain whether a particular site is a purely commercial venture or a purely educational venture. In fact, it might well be the case that no site fits the latter extreme.

Since many websites are produced by unfamiliar sources, the users must look deeper to uncover the bias of an educational website. In addition, unlike in books or films, the information on websites is not static. This can be a strength, allowing site maintainers and authors to continually update material. Hundreds of models for evaluating web sites have been created by university librarians, educational and instructional technologists, and web developers.

Teacher Training in Multicultural Education

In most developing countries, the multicultural education is relatively a new approach. Teacher training is the first priority and it needs to be reorganised in order to improve the capacity of teachers to teach in a multicultural context. The solving of educational problems in the multicultural context cannot be achieved by isolated measures. It is necessary to reshape policies on teacher training and education in order to adapt them to individual-communities' educational needs. The curricula for basic education are frequently mono-cultural.

This situation may reinforce feelings of discrimination among pupils from minorities, which may in turn cause pupils to lose their cultural identity and self-esteem. It is also a cause of low school achievement among pupils from discriminated minorities and thus a big disadvantage for them both in obtaining good jobs and in their integration into society. Appropriate curricula for multicultural/ intercultural education should integrate some of the history and characteristics of all communities.

Teacher training should incorporate strategies and methods that will improve school achievement among pupils from discriminated minorities. Multicultural/intercultural education is a way of reinforcing the cultural identity of pupils from all communities, including those discriminated against. Such education stimulates pupils' self-esteem by developing their knowledge of the characteristics and achievements of their own communities.

Cultural and linguistic diversity is frequently considered to be a negative element in education. However, such diversity can be a resource in classroom activities if teachers are capable of accepting pupils' conceptions and knowledge, and stimulating pupils to share them. Pupils' family life, cultural background and experiences can all be important resources for teachers. Viewing them in this light stimulates pupils' self-esteem, and can help to surmount shyness and discriminatory feelings by developing mutual understanding and solidarity between pupils from different communities.

Multicultural/intercultural education requires the capacity in an educator to adapt teaching to pupils in a learner-centred approach. Some teachers' conceptions and attitudes relating to teaching and learning can obstruct the development of this capacity. For example, teachers frequently think that 'to teach' is identical 'to transmit information' and that 'to learn' is equivalent 'to listen and to remember'. Such teachers are not much concerned by individual pupils' characteristics and do not adapt teaching to pupils' learning difficulties.

Teacher training should help teachers to modify their conceptions so that they may develop the capacity to take into account pupils' characteristics and learning difficulties in a learner-centred approach. Analysis of teachers' conceptions and attitudes about teaching and learning is, therefore, an important element in teacher training. One important element to take into account in teaching is the 'temporal structure' of pupils (monochrone or polychrone). Differences in temporal structures can be a source of misunderstanding between teachers and pupils.

Teacher training should inform teachers about pupils' temporal organisations and develop their capacity to adapt teaching to them. Understanding pupils' learning difficulties is a fundamental element in any educational activity, particularly when the teacher comes from a community other than that of the pupils. Frequently, teachers have problems in communicating with pupils from different cultures. If teachers do not know the precepts of communication used by pupils, they may have difficulty establishing good relations with them. A related problem arises from pupils' taboos. If teachers do not take into account pupils' taboos, they can harm sensibilities and provoke feelings of rejection.

In the multicultural context, analysis of culture and learning difficulties and the strategies and methods for helping pupils overcome the latter are therefore important elements in teacher training. Different cultures have different 'learning styles'. To adapt teaching to pupils' learning styles can facilitate learning and solve some of the pupils' difficulties. Pupils are ethnocentric and frequently have negative attitudes and conceptions about other cultural and ethnic groups.

Pupils' language development is a fundamental educational issue in the multicultural context. Children who have limited capacity in the teaching language have many difficulties achieving proficiency. This situation increases the probability of poor school achievement. Of particular concern is the situation of children coming from families with impoverished language skills or migrant children who lack the opportunity to speak either their mother language or the dominant language fluently.

Effective multilingual education requires the participation of all teachers. Education for sustainable development, adapted to improve the quality of life in different communities, can help solve these problems. One important objective is to improve the capacity to negotiate and the capacity for organising collective activities. This is another example of the possible integration of education towards sustainable development with multicultural/ intercultural education. Multicultural education needs a community-centred approach. Therefore, teacher training needs to include the imparting of basic information about ethnic and cultural groups, such as traditional knowledge, religion, taboos, language, social organisation, communication precepts, temporal organisation, etc.

However, it is important to avoid stereotypes about communities frequently transmitted by teachers; these are an obstacle to an understanding of pupils' problems. Teacher training should develop the capacity for using the basic information about pupils' communities while developing teachers' capacity for adapting teaching to real, unstereotyped pupils. Each community has its own empirical knowledge, which is transmitted to new generations through tales, stories, songs, proverbs, etc. It is important to encourage the integration of traditional knowledge in teaching (in particular in science teaching) as it facilitates learning, allows pupils to learn about their own community, develops cultural identity and self-esteem and permits the conservation of empirical knowledge that would otherwise be lost.

Teacher training should develop a teacher's capacity for establishing good communications with the families of pupils from different communities, and for stimulating them to participate more actively in school activities. Training materials are frequently mono-cultural, presenting only a 'dominant ethnic and cultural model'. Such material may harm the feelings of pupils from minorities and can reinforce discriminatory conceptions and attitudes. Multicultural education needs training material presenting all cultures and the history of all communities.

This training can provide teachers with concepts and methods for developing pupils' capacity for managing conflicts and for stimulating active participation by pupils in solving peacefully any conflicts between communities. Multicultural/intercultural education needs precise information about pupils' communities. This information should be kept updated in order to trace the cultural, social and economic changes in different communities.

A well-organised system of research and transmission of information is an important element in multicultural/intercultural education. This information will allow teaching to be adapted to pupils' difficulties. In the multicultural context, therefore, teachers should be capable not only of establishing good communications with their pupils, but should also have an 'open mind' and a 'scientific approach to teaching'.

Training for Intercultural Bilingual Education

The intercultural bilingual education means to transform the current education system so as to meet the basic learning needs of indigenous learners, and not merely the introduction of an innovation into one specific aspect of the system. The complexity of intercultural bilingual education presents with a wide range of staff requirements. In order to ensure successful application it is necessary to take training action in fields such as research, planning, curriculum development, educational administration, educational supervision and, of course, teaching and classroom activities.

Such research will establish the training needs of the teachers who will be responsible for implementing the intended innovations. To this type of research should be added evaluation, either conducted while the innovation is being carried out or once it is completed. The interdisciplinary nature of intercultural bilingual education also means that research must cover a number of disciplines such as education, descriptive linguistics, psycho-linguistics, socio-linguistics, social psychology applied to the field of linguistics, cognitive psychology, cultural anthropology, cognitive anthropology, applied or educational linguistics, and bilingual teaching practice, the latter a new and rapidly emerging field.

Educators trained to teach bilingually are needed, and this in turn leads to an urgent need for full professional training programmes. This need is not just for training in basic skills to overcome situations caused by inadequate—because it was thought universal and homogeneous—teacher training received in the past. There is a basic requirement for teachers with the ability to guide the learning of mother tongues and a second language, exploiting both the languages and the subordinate and dominant cultures as teaching resources. In view of the undeniable importance of having teachers so trained, it is also important that there should be trainers of trainers: those who will take responsibility for teacher training, so that the innovation takes root at classroom level and teachers' practices are changed.

This new concept of training, which will play a major role in the implementation of innovations at classroom level. In order for bilingual education to succeed, traditional training has to be substantially transformed, because, in many cases, the radical ideas of bilingual education do not outweigh tradition. Training based on exhaustive knowledge of teachers' real practices can thus be provided to modify their performance in the classroom.

In the running of bilingual education programmes, the participation of teachers — indigenous and others — in tasks which are seen as priorities, such as developing new textbooks and guides for children and teachers, has been in response to various requirements. In order to be effective, programmes have generally included in their design a training element to fill gaps in the areas of linguistics, anthropology and teaching, and in matters of ideology and politics.

In the case of intercultural bilingual education, training is not only a question of teaching practice but also of teachers' vision and individual behaviour in the face of diversity. This means that the teacher factor has become one of the main problems of intercultural bilingual education programmes and that training alone is no panacea, since change has also to take place in the affective domain and in teachers' perceptions of themselves and of the world around them.

There was no other solution but to adopt the pattern which is characteristic of every intercultural bilingual education programme today, if several activities are to be carried out simultaneously—research, curriculum development, textbook production, distribution, community work, and so on, i.e. by substantially reducing the time devoted to training. Programmes still face growing problems, given that every training activity has to start by training the intercultural bilingual education teachers in writing the indigenous language—which they usually speak but cannot write—so as to reawaken their linguistic awareness and interest them in studying the language that they will use as the medium of education.

Training needs are greater still if indigenous young people with limited schooling are selected as teachers; this is frequently the case among small indigenous ethnic groups in the region. In such cases, the responsibility goes beyond training itself and has to take into account complementary schooling courses so that the young people at least complete secondary education. This is a situation that affects the implementation of intercultural bilingual education programmes among most indigenous peoples

Every intercultural bilingual education programme to have a more direct influence on teacher training, and it might even be preferable to initiate every intercultural bilingual education programme from a teacher training centre. In that way, the innovation might be more sure of continuity since, by becoming involved in the development of an experimental programme, the teacher training college or institute of education would face the challenge of constantly modifying its practice and the training which it provides for future teachers.

CULTURAL ISSUES IN INTERNATIONAL DISTANCE EDUCATION

The international delivery of distance education can be carried even further into an altruistic one, in that marketing distance education courses internationally provides skills and knowledge that would otherwise not be available in the recipient countries, and helps improve the quality of education in these countries. This in turn helps their economic and social development. These international courses are available only to those that can afford them or have access to the technology, namely, those already privileged within a poorer country.

Developing programmes for international delivery can also enable institutions to prepare their students for an increasingly global economy and society, if courses are planned from the start with an international focus, especially if they involve contributions from or joint development with institutions in other countries. Programmes that have not only students but teachers from other countries studying and teaching collaboratively can provide a strong international perspective that would be difficult to achieve in other ways.

There are many different reasons for offering distance education courses internationally. Institutions though should be clear as to their primary motivation, as that will influence the kind of arrangements that will be most appropriate for international delivery or partnership. In particular, benefits should be apparent for both the providers and the recipients, whether they are individuals or institutions. English is at the moment by far and away the most predominant language in terms of the international delivery of distance education

Online courses though also have some advantages over face-to-face teaching for students working in another language than their own. The asynchronous nature of online teaching allows students to take their time in composing responses in another language, whereas in classroom contexts often the conversation moves on before they have crafted an appropriate intervention. The problem is that providing distance education courses in a foreign language is not just a technical issue. As well as the actual language, such courses come with alien social and cultural contexts.

There are also cultural differences in the approach to teaching. In other cultures, there is great respect shown by students for the teacher, and it is culturally alien to challenge the teacher or even express an opinion on a topic. The online courses aimed at an international audience is that this merely widens the gap between the rich and poor in developing countries, as only the rich have access to the internet.

There are many different ways in which people can access the internet, without owning their own computers or having their own internet accounts. One advantage of working with partner institutions such as universities in other countries is that they usually have internet access and computer facilities on campus, which may be available for student use. Many employers have computers with internet access for work purposes, and may allow or encourage employees to use this for improving their skills and knowledge.

Internet access will get both cheaper and more accessible in developing countries, and it could be argued that it will be to the advantage of people in developing countries to access knowledge and experience of internet learning as quickly as possible. One of the major advantages of online courses is the opportunity for course participants to work collaboratively. However, some students have objected to working collaboratively. Some object to the principle of collaborative learning, irrespective of the nationality of the other students; they believe that they should be assessed solely on their own work, and feel that their grades may be adversely affected by working with someone who is not as 'able' or motivated.

In short, international distance education programmes can raise some interesting and challenging issues. However, a number of strategies can be developed to deal with these issues.

i) It is important to be clear about an institution's motivation in moving into international distance education. If the main reason is to internationalise the curriculum and expose one's own students to other cultural standards, then this will affect the design of the curriculum and the kind of arrangements one wants to make with other institutions. If the aim is to make money, then the approach to curriculum design and partnership is likely to be very different.

ii) There are clearly many benefits to be gained by working in partnership with institutions in different countries, rather than just direct marketing, although direct marketing may still be the only viable option if suitable partners cannot be found.

iii) It will help to have letters of agreement or contracts that spell out clearly expectations and assumptions, division of responsibilities, and financial arrangements, before programmes are developed or delivered.

iv) If possible, programmes should be either designed from scratch with an international market in mind, and/or tailored to local needs. While this may add to the cost of development, it may also result in increased revenues.

v) International distance education programmes should also be available to one's own students, so they can benefit from the international perspective.

vi) Build local capacity for distance education through training contracts. Many institutions in developing countries may be happy to take courses from other countries initially, but most want to develop their own capacity for distance education. Delivery of courses developed elsewhere can be combined with local training.

vii) Some institutions cannot offer whole programmes at a distance because of Senate regulations requiring at least some attendance on campus. This regulation might be waived for international students, so that a whole program can be taken at a distance.

viii) Develop special programmes for course developers to increase sensitivity to intercultural and design issues for programs being delivered internationally.

ix) Perhaps most important of all, identify the unique contributions that each partner institution can make to the development and delivery of international programmes, so that all parties can clearly see the benefits.

References

Amadio, M., "Two decades of bilingual education", *Prospects,* UNESCO, Paris, vol. XX, no. 3, 1990, p. 343-41.

Bates, Tony, *Cultural and ethical issues in international distance education*", Director, Distance Education and Technology, Continuing Studies, The University of British Columbia

Bartolic, S. and Bates, A.W., "Investing in online learning: potential benefits and limitations", *Canadian Journal of Communication,* Vol. 24, No.3, 1999.

Bates, A.W, and Escamilla, J., "Crossing Boundaries: Making Global Distance Education a Reality", *Journal of Distance Education,* Vol.12, Nos. 1&2, pp. 49-66, 1997.

Ferguson, T., "Communicating in the multilingual classroom", In: MacGregor, M., Moore, R., eds. *Tetrting mathematics in the multiculturul classroom : a resource for teachers and teacher educutors*, Melbourne, Australia, School of Science and Mathematics Education, Institute of Education, The University of Melbourne, 1991.

Gorski, Paul, *Multicultural Education and the Internet: Tools, Resources, and Commentary,* Founder and Site Author of the Multicultural Pavilion, September,1999.

Hafner, A.L., Spencer Green, J., "Multicultural education and diversity: providing information to teachers", Annual meeting of the American Association of Colleges of Teacher Education (San Antonio, TX), 1992

Hall, E.T., "Making sense without words", In: Fersh, S., ed. *Learning about peoples und cultures,* Evanston, McDougal, Litell, 1974.

McDiarmid, G.W., *What's the matter? Preparing teachers for culturally diverse classrooms,* Reno, NV, Far West Region Holmes Group, 1989.

Zeichner, K., "Educating teachers for cultural diversity", *East Lansing,* MI, Michigan State University, National Center for Research on Teacher Education, 1992.

4

Teaching with and about New Technologies

Long before computers and the internet, radio and TV had arrived in schools. From the early 1950s, educational radio programmes were used in classrooms and relayed by teachers almost everywhere in Latin America, Asia and Africa. More recently, Indonesia has used radio to reach school children scattered in the country's outlying islands. In the 1990s, with help from UNESCO, Mongolia used radio to show women how to set up and run small businesses. The educational possibilities of TV were also widely seized on but with very mixed results.

In 1960, China became the first country to use TV and radio for distance learning in higher education. In the 1970s, many thought these media could improve education in developing countries, and international organisations supported production of televised secondary school courses, notably in Côte d'Ivoire and El Salvador. But the results were disappointing. Teachers did not like such interference by the central government and the new methods were very costly.

Today, new information and communication technologies (ICTs) really a turning point in the field of education. "ICTs have not eliminated the most pressing problems that education systems face," comments Vladimir Kinelev, Director of the UNESCO Institute for Information Technologies in Education (IITE). The problem, he says, is that "attempts to improve education through the use of ICTs suffer from the absence of sound education paradigms that could support genuine renewal."

However, the new technologies are certainly quite different from earlier media. Internet penetration of schools has actually been spectacular. The arrival of the worldwide web also greatly boosted distance learning. For schools the benefits are twofold: it's a tool that helps learning and it also gives children key skills for the job market because, unlike TV and radio, it calls for special abilities. These are indispensable skills in the future information society. The problem is that ICTs, the backbone of globalisation, are still the reserve of rich countries. In many countries, girls are kept away from new technologies, just as they are kept out of school. In 2001, only 22 per cent of internet users in Asia were women, 38 per cent in Latin America and just 6 per cent in the Middle East. Even in rich countries, where ICTs have been in classrooms for several years now, things are far from ideal.

The rapid advance of information technology is driving shifts in every other form of societal institution, in ways that are often unplanned and sometimes unfortunate. The development of the internet is fostering the creation and proliferation of emerging interactive media, such as the web and shared virtual environments. A medium is in part a channel for conveying content; as the internet increasingly pervades society, university instructors can readily reach extensive, remote resources and audiences on-demand, just-in-time. Just as important, however, a medium is a representational container enabling new types of messages. Since expression and communication are based on representations such as language and imagery, the process of learning is enhanced by broadening the types of instructional messages students and faculty can exchange.

Central to the effective utilisation of emerging educational technologies via distributed learning is developing a reflective understanding of how each interactive medium shapes the cognitive, affective, and social interactions of participants. The creation, sharing, and mastery of knowledge is not simply an intellectual exercise;

the emotional and psychosocial dimensions of learning are very important as well. Emerging interactive media enable an extraordinary range of cognitive, affective, and social "affordances" (enhancements of human capabilities) of great power for distributed learning while at the same time also potentially limiting students' and instructors' expression and communication.

Technology is driving the demand for new forms of higher education because the pace of change in the workplace is requiring adults to be constantly retrained. Education, and associated credentials certifying learning, will increasingly be required on an ongoing basis as our workplace evolves with ever-increasing change. Technology in post secondary education affords the opportunity to create a learning environment that is learner-centric, individualised, and interactive.

Internet-based education offers the potential of thousands of classes on hundreds of subjects available any time night or day, at any place, at the convenience of the student. Although post secondary education has been both place-bound and time-bound, the source of knowledge and learning has traditionally been the professor. Knowledge and learning is now available over the internet.

In the former, teachers are presumed to be the font of all wisdom and knowledge. Their job is to move that wisdom and knowledge from their own brains to the receiver brains of their students. Almost nothing is taken into account regarding the personal context, knowledge, or experience that each learner already brings to the learning situation. Students are seen primarily as empty vessels or passive receptacles waiting to be filled.

Some universities will develop a "brick-and-click" approach by offering a combination of classroom courses, on line courses, and hybrid courses that combine on line teaching with classroom discussion, as well as offering on line courses through their continuing education departments to reach out to other learners. However, the use of technology does not change the fundamental distinctions between the traditional educational system and the new models of online learning. Those distinctions are in the role of the student, the role of faculty, and the role of the institution.

The new models of online education serve different functions than the traditional universities. Fundamentally, online education is more applicable to lifelong learning than to education as an event, and it is more applicable to working adults than to students just out of high school. Online learning implies learner-centric education, where learners take responsibility to choose learning activities of most value and relevance to them. The potential of online learning cannot be realised without addressing some significant challenges.

The major challenges to distance education during the past 50 years have been low student completion rates and the lack of collaboration one would experience in a campus environment with both faculty and other students. However, internet-based education can potentially address both of these issues. Collaboration over the internet, using chat rooms, threaded discussion groups, message boards, and other tools, may be even richer than the interactions on campus. Increased collaboration leads to a sense of a learning community, and as a result, higher completion rates.

Educational Technologies of the New age

Online learning is the new generation in the evolutionary growth of open, flexible and distance learning. Today, internet users represented barely seven per cent of the global population. To ensure widespread access to online learning programmes in many parts of the world, it is often necessary and cost-effective to build digital "bridges" into their design.

The internet, the backbone of online learning, is an interlinked network of networks that allows computers worldwide to connect to it, and to communicate or exchange data with each other. The internet is based on Transmission Control Protocol – Internet Protocol (TCP/IP); information is routed in "packets" according to TCP/IP specifications. The

WWW works on the internet through its own HyperText Transfer Protocol (HTTP), an interactive platform that uses the following media:

i) Text, plain or formatted
ii) Hybrid text/graphics documents, such as Adobe Acrobat
iii) Colour images, still and animated or videos
iv) Sound
v) 3-D models

Preparing text-based learning material is relatively easy and can be done with only computer keyboarding skills. Text-based materials are also easily accessed and understood by learners. A typical web page is prepared using HyperText Markup Language (HTML) instructions; HTML files can be created using common word processing software, such as Microsoft Word. The WWW also supports other text formats, such as Rich Text Format (.RTF) or Adobe Acrobat's Portable Document Format (.PDF), which can be embedded within HTML-coded pages.

Graphics and images can be created, or digitised using a scanner and imported into a computer using specific image manipulation software, such as Adobe PhotoShop or Adobe Illustrator. Images are then imported into an HTML web page. Common image formats include the Graphic Interchange Format (.GIF) and Joint Experts Photography Group (.JEPG), which use compression technology to make image file sizes smaller for quicker web display or download.

Though graphics and images are useful learning tools, their preparation requires some skill and experience in using graphic design software. Graphics or images generally have a bigger file size than plain text, and take longer to download or to display on screen. Hazardous and costly experiments can be captured using video for presentation on the WWW, for repeated use. With new digital audio and video progressive download and streaming capabilities, audio and video can be transmitted directly over the internet although transmission quality still depends on the learner's network connection and available bandwidth.

Popular audio and video file formats and software include Apple Quick Time, Windows Media Technologies and RealNetwork's Real Systems. Another emerging format is the Motion Pictures Experts Group (.MPEG), although the disadvantage of MPEG is that the whole file must be downloaded before it starts to play. If high bandwidth is available, all these technologies can deliver high quality video and sound.

The WWW animation standard is animated GIF files, although Java, Shockwave and Macromedia Flash are also used. The standard for 3-D modelling is Virtual Reality Modelling Language (VRML). A web browser needs a VRML plug-in to display 3-D models properly. Designing quality animation and 3-D models also requires a high degree of skills and experience in the appropriate software.

Designing online learning requires grounding in pedagogy, an understanding of the subject to be taught and of how the WWW works. Online learning can be a supplement to face-to-face instruction, equally mixed with face-to-face instruction, or the main delivery method, instead of face-to-face instruction. The last category is the most challenging for educators and instructional designers. When designing online learning, it is best to consider the best practices of all learning theories (behaviourism, cognitivism, constructivism). The WWW provides opportunities to use all these.

Interaction is a major contributing factor to successful learning experiences. Assessment and evaluation of learner performance is crucial. Although online examination brings a number of authenticity, security and certification issues, evaluation models should take the WWW's constructivist (student-centred) approach into account. The WWW can facilitate many evaluation systems – from computer-based (web-based) objective testing to tutor-evaluated, long answer tests or assignments – but is capable of supporting much more than the traditional, three-hour paper and pencil test.

Online course developers now use alternative assessment tools such as evidence-based tests (where learners submit projects online), learning diary submission, participation in discussion forums or peer-based evaluation. The nature of online learning requires learners to be very self-motivated. The role of the instructor is to challenge learner curiosity and help learners achieve personal learning goals. Online learning should therefore be designed according to adult learning principles, in which learners have as much responsibility as their teachers, if not more.

Learners need to be informed of their role and responsibility prior to starting the course. A period of orientation may be needed, as most online learners are initially novices of the medium. At this point in the design and development of online learning, most institutions and instructors have to decide if the course will be developed using a suite of individually available web tools, or an integrated course delivery software package.

In general, web-based applications such as email, discussion groups and chat software are not designed for educational purposes. Using them in isolation or developing an integrated educational system around them may not be effective in terms of cost, time or learning outcomes. Integrated systems for online learning are needed because the generic web environment does not provide:

i) a standard way to organise course materials
ii) prior evidence of the environment's instructional effectiveness
iii) tools to support basic instructional activities such as course design, organisation of groups spaces and personal spaces, grading, and easy integration of multiple media files
iv) models to support learning strategies that involve collaborative learning, knowledge building and multiple representations of ideas and knowledge structures.

Integrated application software packages include facilities for every aspect of designing an online learning programme. Following are the learner tools when they log on to the system:

i) *Course tools*: for content presentation, displaying industry-standard, interactive web pages to learners. The pages have links for navigation, and contain all course texts, graphics and multimedia learning materials

ii) *Collaboration tools*: for synchronous and asynchronous activities like email for one-to-one communication, discussion boards for conferencing, chat for real time clarification of doubts, whiteboards for lecture presentation and group work, or a virtual "drop box" for sharing programmes and applications

iii) *Support tools*: include personal learner profiles, a facility to upload files to the system (e.g., for submitting assignments), personal library, search facilities, study skills guidance, bookmark facilities and calendars.

iv) *Developer tools* for the website administrator and the instructor. These seem initially more complex, but are easy to use after a short training or demonstration period:

v) *Administrator tools*: allow course software to be installed on a server, provides resource monitoring and website management facilities. Assigns user identification, passwords and usage rights to learners. Some systems also handle online registration and fee payment

vi) *Designer tools*: online teaching tools for the instructor. Includes facilities to prepare course plans, upload files (course content) and announcements, design assessment tools (such as quizzes) and a calendar of activities. The instructor can also design the appearance of individual web pages through choice of background colour, text font and type of images or graphics.

Learning management tools are features to track student progress and log-ins to the website. Instructors can monitor the progress of individual learners and provide personalised feedback. Complete statistics on website use can be generated for reviewing or evaluating policies and practices.

Educational Applications of Broadband Technologies

Broadband applications are driving demand for bandwidth. The growing demand for broadband in education reflects the strategic importance of broadband technologies for education delivery—the education sector will increasingly deliver services through broadband channels. Broadband will enable educators to realise key policy objectives in the schools sector, in Vocational Education and Training (VET) and in higher education.

Education institutions do not have the capacity to make the large capital investments that a comprehensive broadband infrastructure requires. A significant issue related to take-up is the need for professional development programmes, both to equip staff with the skills to use broadband applications and to enable staff to explore the potential uses and innovations that broadband can deliver. Other barriers to broadband uptake in education include cultural change issues, the need for technical support and bandwidth management problems.

Some initiatives currently in progress aim to increase broadband capacity in schools. Many schools that are upgrading their bandwidth still cannot access broadband applications, because the number of connected devices reduces their effective bandwidth. Schools are well advanced with the integration of ICT and e-learning into their curriculums, but the provision and use of high-speed broadband connections is at a relatively early stage.

'E-learning' initiatives encompass a wide set of applications and processes, using all available electronic media to deliver education. They include computer-based learning, web-based learning, virtual classrooms and digital collaboration. Online learning is a subset of these e-learning projects that uses the internet, intranets and extranets. Broadband technologies enable many of these online learning applications.

Adult learners have pressing demands on their time. A flexible learning environment facilitates good outcomes for students. VET institutions are implementing programmes to address flexible learning needs and for some years, they have placed an emphasis on developing online content. Online content developed in the VET sector forms packages that include collections of resources, suggested learning strategies and supporting material. The VET sector has integrated these online learning tools into its courses to complement face-to-face delivery.

Poor connectivity represents a major barrier to any media-rich, interactive online learning experiences across the VET system. Different content developers approach the issue of variable or insufficient broadband in different ways. Some developers choose to take full advantage of the greatest bandwidth available in the sector, using video, audio and graphics. These developers accept that not all institutions have access to high bandwidth. They believe that if institutions and jurisdictions have difficulty using high bandwidth content, it will force them to address their supply problems.

The bandwidth problems currently facing content developers and institutions can be addressed by increasing bandwidth through improved broadband availability and pricing. The higher education sector has considerably greater access to bandwidth than other education sub-sectors. Online learning is among the most compelling applications for broadband technology in the higher education sector.

Broadband can transform the learning experience for students as it can expose them to a range of exciting and innovative learning content that was previously either inaccessible or unpractical in the narrowband environment. The benefits of broadband is that it can facilitate and enhance inter-institutional collaboration. For example, broadband can be used to share scarce teacher resources between schools and colleges via high-speed interactive videoconferencing; it can also be used to link different institutions to create innovative joint projects that encourage communication and cooperation.

Broadband can also facilitate new and innovative e-learning opportunities on a wider scale. Broadband can deliver real efficiencies in existing provision by streamlining reporting and administration as well as automating the administration and management of educational institutions.

Broadband can also be exploited to widen access to educational material and new learning opportunities by using links from schools to the wider communities, such as libraries, museums, theatres and other cultural institutions. Broadband is also used as a means of widening access in rural areas and providing access to education materials to learners with disabilities or behavioural problems.

Despite the many good examples of progress being made in the application of broadband within the education sector, most teachers are still not fully exploiting the potential of ICT in the classroom. The introduction of ICT represents a major systemic change to the traditional methods of teaching and learning and therefore needs to be accompanied by effective change management to ensure that all stakeholders feel motivated and reassured to want to use it.

Governments have a key role to play in this change management process by ensuring that the benefits of using broadband within education are evangelised, incentivised and supported right throughout the education value chain. As a part of this change management process, a number of issues will need to be addressed. These include:

i) motivating users and decision makers to ensure that the deployment of broadband becomes an educational 'pull' rather than a technology 'push';
ii) addressing inconsistencies in the use of broadband across the education system, to ensure that benefits are delivered as widely as possible;

iii) overcoming the fragmentation of funding streams available so that innovative broadband projects can be more easily supported; and

iv) making sure that broadband projects, which often involve long term infrastructure investments are structured on a more sustainable basis.

The full support and buy-in of educational leaders and decision makers is critical to ensure the widespread adoption and use of broadband in education. While leaders and decision makers are interested in how broadband can transform the structural and operational performance of their organisations, they are also under pressure to achieve value for money and to meet the targets set by government and their own governance bodies. They therefore need to be reassured and motivated before they commit additional resources to broadband within their organisation.

Educators and learning facilitators need to have a clear understanding of how broadband can help them do their job more efficiently and effectively. Whilst many are already using ICT quite extensively, others remain either unaware or unconvinced about the benefits that ICT and broadband in particular can deliver. Evidence suggests that pupils who use ICT in the classroom get better results than those who don't and there is an emerging range of broadband specific educational content and learning packages that can greatly enhance the learning experience and support the pedagogy.

However, it will be necessary to make sure that educators buy-in to these benefits if they are to be motivated to incorporate them in to their daily teaching activities. Broadband needs to be an educational 'pull' rather than a technology 'push' if the full benefits of its use are to be achieved. Explaining how broadband can enable educators and learning facilitators to teach and assess their students more efficiently will be key to the broadband adoption process in education.

However, there is also an issue around appropriate technical support in the use of these technologies to ensure that the technology does not impose undue burden on educators and learning facilitators and divert their attention away from teaching. In order to provide appropriate technological support, leaders and decision makers need to consider and plan resourcing ICT support requirements in the context of increasingly sophisticated broadband networks.

Parents and mentors who take a strong interest in their children's education are likely to be motivated to embrace a technology if they are convinced of its relevance to their children's education. For example, most parents would agree that a PC is advantageous to their children's education however, in order to motivate parents to embrace broadband they need to be convinced of the real additional value that it brings to the PC, i.e., the content and services that it makes available to the learner and the potential to collaborate.

Most learners are reasonably receptive to new technologies, however they need to feel motivated to want to use them and therefore the expectations of their teachers/ lecturers will influence their level of motivation. For example, as home PCs became more pervasive there was a growing expectation from educators in the higher education sector that student assignments should be submitted in typed format rather than handwritten. This change was significant for many who were not used to typing, let alone used to using the technology.

There are a variety of reasons why this change took place however, students are clearly strongly motivated to present their assignment in the best possible light and not be disadvantaged compared to his/her fellow students. The same can be said about broadband.

Even where broadband is being used to support the pedagogy or administration, evidence suggests that it is rarely applied strategically to all of the processes within individual institutions. The failure to fully integrate broadband within educational institutions will impact on the ability to deliver on educational targets, and in fact, even the setting of these targets.

Public and private partnerships are clearly important for developing innovative broadband projects within education.

However, the lack of sustainability (i.e., the ability of a project to be self-sufficient once the initial funding has stopped) and replicability (i.e., that it should be possible to replicate elements of the project elsewhere) within project funding models is of paramount concern. If the use of ICT and broadband in education is to increase, the ICT support structures available to education institutions need to be strengthened.

Challenges of E-learning Environments

The enrichment of the learning environment through ICTs depend on several factors:

i) political and financial willingness to invest in new technology;
ii) up-to-date infrastructure, computers, data networks accessible to the public;
iii) information campaigns;
iv) suitability of teaching and learning materials for adults;
v) more resources for households to spend on the internet;
vi) networks providing opportunities for all adults to get familiar with ICT;
vii) partnership between educational institutions and cultural services.

While new information technologies might help improvement in the quality of higher education, it has to be underscored that universal literacy and the spread of education, including post-elementary adult education, are a prerequisite for information technologies to be an effective agent of social transformation. New information technologies can offer learning opportunities complementary to and/or continuous with mass media, in particular, radio and television. These are being used in several parts of Asia and Africa to promote adult learning, to reduce the cultural barriers to participate in education and to disseminate information on the range of opportunities.

There are four criteria for policy makers for the use of technologies in education systems:

i) the choice of new technologies that are efficient for broadcast media, while at the same time allowing for interaction;
ii) their integration into an overall educational strategy;
iii) appropriation of these new technologies;
iv) mastery of the tools by educational personnel.

The use of new technologies raises many problems:

i) insufficient attention to the interactive aspects of learning;
ii) alienation of the people from their everyday social life and local context;
iii) new technologies relying heavily on written communication;
iv) adults not being sufficiently prepared for new technology; technology not yet adapted to mass learning;
v) lack of trained local mentors.

It is not enough to put good computers and internet connections in classrooms. They have to be used properly. This means schools must change their methods and find new ways to convey knowledge. ICTs will be little use if they simply produce electronic versions of existing books or put classroom lessons online. The internet, digital TV and electronic publishing can take things much further along. Teachers, who can now be emailed out of school hours, also have to adapt.

A lot of mistakes have been made introducing ICTs in schools. Some countries have bought an enormous amount of equipment without realising how very different the technology is. Teachers have to be trained not only to use the tool but also to change the way they teach. New technologies have great promise and can revolutionise learning but only if those involved give themselves the means to do so. Like any tool, it all depends on what people do with it.

The e-learning strategy should help to shape a vision of future learning, and suggests how the vision can be realised. The strategy is founded on a basic principle of universal excellence for learners and teachers in all sectors and organisations. Universal excellence will not happen without co-ordination across the public sector, as new technology needs to operate at scale, to specified standards, in order to be economical.

At the heart of the strategy is the aim to realise the full potential of digital technology through its effective use and embed it in all our learning and teaching processes. The strategy consultation process should engage all stakeholders in debating what e-learning can offer them, what role they can play in embedding e-learning, and what kind of support they need to do it. The proposed strategic actions will impact in different ways:

i) *For a head teacher:* The strategy makes it clear that e-learning is here to stay, as it offers more creative ways of teaching, and engages young people in more active learning. The strategy recognises the barriers that exist, and shows how heads might be supported in the difficult transition to embedded e-learning. A coherent procurement process would save staff time, along with advice on investment planning over the long term

ii) *For a principal or vice chancellor:* The support for leaders in planning and managing e-learning would enable colleges to cover a broader curriculum by linking up with other colleges to provide access to minority subjects. The focus on moving to more e-enabled assessment on demand would be responsive to what young people want, and help with retention and inclusion

To empower learners we need an education workforce that can adapt to change, and has the skills and confidence to exploit e-learning to the full in an everchanging environment. The whole of the education and training workforce must be fully engaged in order to lead change and deliver effective e-learning. This means high-quality initial training and professional development. All teachers, lecturers, tutors, pre-school carers, teaching assistants, learning support assistants, adult and community support staff, mentors, trainers—all professionals and voluntary workers coming into contact with learners.

References

Baily, M., "Great expectations: PCs and productivity," In: R. Kling (editor). *Computerisation and Controversy.* San Diego: Academic Press, p. 21, 1996.

Bonk, C.J, & King, K.S., "Computer conferencing and collaborative writing tools: Starting a dialogue about student dialogue", In C.J. Bonk, & K.S. King (Eds.), *Electronic Collaborators: Learner-centered technologies for literacy, apprenticeship, and discourse*, Mahwah, NJ: Erlbaum, in press, 1998.

Brookfield, S., *Becoming a Critically Reflective Teacher*, San Francisco: Jossey-Bass, p. 6, 1995.

Crook, C., *Computers and the collaborative experience of learning*, Routledge: London & New York, 1994.

Graumann, C.F., "Commonality, mutuality, reciprocity: A conceptual introduction", In I. Markova, C. Graumann & K. Foppa (Eds.), *Mutualities in dialogue* (pp. 1-24), New York, Cambridge University Press, 1995.

Hiltz, S.R., *The virtual classroom: Learning without limits via computer networks*, Norwood NJ: Ablex, Human-computer Interaction series, 1994.

Kerry T, and Tollitt-Evans, J., *Teaching in Further Education*, Oxford: Blackwell, p. 120, 1990.

Khan, B.H., Ed., *Web-based instruction*, Englewood Cliffs, NJ: Educational Technology Publications, 1997.

Kiesler, S., Siegel, J. & McGuire, T.W., "Social psychological impacts of computer-mediated communication", *American Psychologist*, 39(10), 1123-1134, 1984.

Koschmann, T.D., "Toward a theory of computer support for collaborative learning", *Journal of Learning Sciences*, 3(3), 219-225, 1994.

Merseth, K., "Supporting beginning teachers with computer networks", *Journal of Teacher Education*, 42, 140-147, 1991

Mendenhall, Robert W., *Technology: Creating New Models in Higher Education*, Western Governors University.

Scigliano J, and Levin, J., "One-stop shopping in an online educational mall," *T.H.E. (Technological Horizons in Education) Journal*, volume 27, number 11 June, 2000.

Shrum, L., "Introducing Teachers to Telecommunications: California's (ESTTI)," *T.H.E. (Technological Horizons in Education) Journal, volume 15,* number 8, April, 1998

Whittle, D., *Cyberspace: The Human Dimension*, New York: W.H. Freeman, p. 37, 1998.

5

Online Teaching Tools

Technology is being used in education as a tool for learning, collaboration, curriculum development, and staff development. The only real measure of the effectiveness of technologies and technology-enhanced educational programmes is the extent to which they promote and support students' engaged learning and collaboration. Issues of learning and technology are more critical today than ever before. To meet new challenges, educational decision makers need information about technology—its cost effectiveness, how it delivers information, and its accessibility.

Technologies are still very expensive. Decision makers must understand differences in cost, capabilities, use, and effectiveness among various technologies and technology-based programmes in order to spend their limited dollars wisely. Technology changes how information and resources get to schools and other agencies. Electronic publishing allows many different kinds of information providers to serve schools.

Printed textbooks may no longer be schools' primary sources of content. This reconfiguration must be planned with the learning goals for students as the top priority. Access to technology and technology-enhanced programmes must be equitable, and not promulgate and extend differences in educational quality among schools. Decision makers must ensure that poor schools, especially those with students who are academically at risk, have the same opportunities to access and use technologies as schools that are financially better off.

Distance learning technologies traditionally employ one-way video with two-way audio, two-way audio/video, or two-way audio and/or audio graphics to present instruction or information not otherwise available to remote locations.

The next generation of distance education technologies must promote engaged learning. And, in fact, both distance learning providers and models are evolving to this end. Already, more distance learning programmes are using interactive and networked designs that use computers, telephones, videos, facsimiles, audiographics, and other technologies.

The internet is fast becoming the nation's major vehicle for distance education at all levels. The internet makes available resources and information previously accessible only by satellite, video, or in person. World Wide Web (WWW) browsers, such as Mosaic or Netscape, transport video and voice images and support distance education. The internet's access to digital libraries that offer collections of art, historical papers, and other unique or rare items on demand are also powerful tools for distance education.

Telecommunication Technologies as Teaching Tools

Telecommunications resources are becoming more readily available in schools by using telecommunications technologies as tools for professional development. Teachers with in-school access to modems, computers and phone lines may be searching for useful curricular resources, engaging their students in pen-pal relationships with other schools or in multi-site science or social studies investigations, and exchanging email with friends and relatives in distant parts of the globe.

There are a number advantages in building virtual learning communities for teachers. Telecommunications affords teachers the option of communicating with colleagues at times which are convenient to them. The asynchronous nature of communication in this medium means that teachers can establish a rhythm for the exchange of ideas that meshes with the routines of their professional and personal lives. Telecommunications offers an environment in which teachers can reflect on the nature of their professional work.

For some teachers, telecommunications expands the horizons of their classroom, opening the doors to real audiences and exciting interactive activities from locations around the country and the world. These teachers know its capacity to motivate students and involve them in productive learning experiences. There are still a myriad of technical obstacles to overcome in preparing to use computers, modems, and phone lines in the classroom.

Most computer using teachers expect instant results as they implement technology: plug the computer in, boot the word processor, and begin writing. Plug the printer in and begin printing. Plug the modem in and dial an information service. They expect to announce their presence on a network, request a "computer pal" and instantly have their students involved in meaningful exchanges. These teachers haven't yet realised that installing their modems, learning their terminal software, and getting connected online are simply the preliminary and easiest parts of their task. Having dealt with these technological components, they must now depend on other people to participate with them in an interactive project.

There are number of guidelines and principles that have led to many successful online learning activities in classrooms. The first rule of successful online learning activities is to avoid starting with the stereotypical pen pal activity. Networking activities can encompass a wide variety of project ideas, especially projects in which students can collect data and information for use by other participants on the network. As teachers gain skill and comfort with networking technology, and as networks become more accessible to both teachers and students, classroom telecomputing technologies will grow in importance as a tool for involving students in interactive projects that will motivate them to improve their skills and learn about the world around them.

Computer Mediated Communication (CMC)

The Computer Mediated Communication (CMC) systems are used for supporting group learning, that is, systems that allow groups to interact over time as well as over geographical location. This is a different type of interaction to that supported by videoconference systems, which allow people to be geographically dispersed, but require them to be present at the same time.

Email, for example, is a simple form of CMC. The main difference between email and a CMC system is that the structure of a discussion is maintained in a coherent model without the user needing to do anything, making it suited to group-based interactions. With email, messages arrive chronologically and are only grouped if the user takes to time to put related messages into folders.

CMC systems allow learners to interact with one another over time. This time independence allows students to fit their on-line discussions around their other commitments and responsibilities. Different work patterns can be supported whilst still maintaining a feeling of community amongst the students and staff participating in the course. This is particularly pertinent where students are distributed around the world and potentially in different time-zones. These systems retain a textual, permanent record of interactions, indicating to a user as they rejoin a discussion which comments have been added since the last time they were there.

Learning in a CMC environment can lead to deeper processing of material because time for reflection is allowed. Due to the textual record that is kept, people can refer back to things that were discussed earlier, and take their time to respond, perhaps researching their answer before putting it online. CMC systems provide opportunities for groupwork that would not otherwise exist, e.g., for distance learning students on programmes where all support is done remotely via mail, email or phone/FAX.

The use of CMC systems to support distance learners has clear advantages of flexibility over the time and place of study. CMC is of course not a panacea. Since it is largely a text-based medium (although increasingly new systems support multimedia), there is a lack of expressive richness since no non-verbal cues exist to enhance what is being said, and in particular the way that something is being said.

Decision making can be difficult online, again due to flexibility over time and the notion that everyone can have their say in this environment. Using CMC systems requires access to a computer and the internet, and arguably participants require a certain level of technical competence to overcome any difficulties that arise from accessing the CMC environment.

The style of online communication has to be developed by the group. Different groups develop different norms and styles as they would in a face-to-face situation, but online communication is different in that it is not formal letter writing and neither is it a postcard. Also the level of discourse may be different for different areas of a CMC system.

CMC allows participants to work in ways that may otherwise be impossible due to constraints of time or location. It is difficult to imagine a student body from different continents, collaborating on the design of a web page for example, in a non-CMC supported distance learning course. Use of CMC allows design discussions and decisions to be made as a group, over time.

The overall aim of the internet as a Tool for Collaborative Learning project was to establish an international student-based learning project around resources found on the internet. A support and discussion network was established using computer-mediated communications (CMC). This network allowed the four teams to engage in electronic discussions and share online multimedia resources. The network was a good medium for students to share things which they found of value and to comment upon such materials.

The international collaboration was intended to promote the articulation and sharing of different viewpoints and contexts/cultural values that can aid 'deeper processing' of information, concept refinement and active engagement in the learning task.

CMC system supporting teaching and learning that both tutors and students commit themselves to spending time online and that they do so visibly, even if it is only leaving a brief message to say that they have read something and will return to it with more comment later. Another critical factor is clarity about the roles that tutors and students are adopting when engaging in this environment. A number of different roles may be adopted over the length of the course, depending on the educational aims. However what follows are some thoughts about the roles that could be adopted.

A CMC environment can allow students to take more control over their learning, initially perhaps just over the time and place of learning. However, it allows all students to have a voice without the need to fight for airtime as in a face-to-face situation. This can allow different students to take the lead at different times, perhaps in a formal way e.g. taking responsibility for starting a particular discussion topic. Depending on the particular educational implementation adopted, it can provide an environment for small group working allowing students to develop valuable group working, collaboration and coordination skills. They can also develop reflexivity as the online environment retains a copy of all interactions and students can be encouraged to revisit material and reflect upon it. There is also an opportunity for peer assessment since all interactions are held online.

Computer Managed Learning (CML)

The difference between a CMC environment and a Computer Managed Learning (CML) environment is the amount of the administration and coordination of a learning event that the system supports. Typically CMC is one part of a complex delivery system that supports a particular learning event. CML environments on the other hand support a wider range of the processes that go into making an educational experience, e.g., schedules, assessments, resources as well as discursive CMC-type elements. Examples of these systems are:

i) WebCT
ii) Lotus' Learning Space

WebCT: This tool facilitates the creation of sophisticated World Wide Web-based educational environments by non-technical users. It can be used to create entire online courses, or to simply publish materials that supplement existing courses. It uses WWW browsers as the interface for the course-building environment. Aside from facilitating the organisation of course material on the web, WebCT also provides a wide variety of tools and features that can be added to a course. Examples of tools include a conferencing system, online chat, student progress tracking, group project organisation, student self-evaluation, grade maintenance and distribution, access control, navigation tools, auto-marked quizzes, electronic mail, automatic index generation, course calendar, student homepages, course content searches.

Lotus' Learning Space: LearningSpace comes with two instructor tools for course management: (i) Assessment Manager (ii) LearningSpace Central. Learning Space allows different resources to be brought together in a single course support environment that is accessible via the WWW.

Computer-Driven Approaches and Educational Software

The technology performance level of computer-driven approaches and educational software varies according to the individual approach and the learning context or purpose to which it is applied. Computer-based instruction (CBI) used for drill and practice on traditional objectives does not engage learners and has low technology performance. On the other hand, computer-based technologies derived from artificial intelligence and research in cognitive science promote engaged learning. Such systems help learners think through complex, authentic problems; take charge of their own learning; and develop products for teaching or use in the real world. These systems integrate media to:

i) provide sophisticated expert systems for learning very complex concepts and procedures;
ii) help students develop advanced skills such as reasoning, summarising, high-level self-questioning, and reflection;
iii) diagnose and reduce student errors and remediate specific learning problems;
iv) adjust or adapt the level and sequence of problems based on student performances and suggest directions for new learning; and
v) simulate the use of emerging technologies and decision making to address complex real-world problems and issues, thereby providing learning by doing and guided participation.

Increasingly, computers will "read" and "think" like humans. When this happens, they will be able to track and respond to complex lines of inquiry. Even now, computers and integrated media can—and frequently do—prompt learners in pursuing more difficult tasks. This means that, when evaluating computer-based technologies, it is important to consider the intelligence or "thinking" the computer can do — as well as its purpose or use in achieving a given instructional or learning goal.

Integrated Learning Systems (ILSs)

Integrated learning systems provide information from a central source using LANs for communication within and between schools. Many schools believe that because they have a high technology performance ILS, they provide engaged learning and access to rich resources. ILSs provide in-service training on the programme's system and content, easy-to-use and time saving management tools, and good support for technology. Some programmes are interdisciplinary and include multimedia encyclopaedias. The fallacy in this thinking, however, lies in the fact that ILSs generally support traditional tasks and assessments, traditional student and teacher roles, and traditional instructional approaches targeted to basic skills.

ILSs' centralised resource configuration also limits their usefulness. LANs, especially with regard to ILS, so far have not produced significant school change. One reason may be that while most schools have the modems that would link them to other education and information sources, their network technology is primarily for downloading instructional materials from a central repository to isolated classrooms. Remedying this limitation requires connecting the LANs to WANs and other distributed systems, including the internet, that provide external resources and opportunities for active learning and communication.

ILSs could support engaged learning in other ways too. For one thing, some ILSs enable schools to access third-party software. Also, some ILSs have multimedia production capabilities that allow teachers to create their own curricular models and allow students to produce an array of documents and other products. A few ILS companies are developing networks outside the system, instructional designs that focus on authentic tasks, and ongoing professional development.

World Wide Web (WWW)

The world wide web is one of the most accessible tools available for academics to use. It allows an easy means of publishing material, it has a low learning-curve, the majority of its browsers are graphical and user-friendly, and above all it is free to most people in higher education. The web works on a client-server principle. The user launches their browser on their machine which in turn interrogates a server retrieving files. Files are located via their Uniform Resource Locator (URL)—a unique address detailing the protocol for transferring the data, the domain name of the web server, and the pathname/filename of the actual document.

The web can be viewed as one enormous resource that is interlinked, but ever expanding. The problem then is not so much the lack of resources, but more that of locating them, the needle in the pile of needles. Two approaches to solving this problem have developed over the years. The first is the use of gateways, the second the use of search engines. Gateways are not the only way of locating existing web pages, but they do provide the advantage of being subject specific and selective. However, it is possible that the Gateways in existence do not cover your subject area in any great detail.

Internet Search engines have existed since the early days of the web. Many users clearly do not know how to use the query language inherent in most search engines. Before moving on to looking at the types of things academics are using the web for in teaching, it is useful to confront some of the common problems users of the web encounter. The web works under a hypertext metaphor, i.e., it operates via a series of nodes and links. Therefore, when using the web for instructive purposes the academic has to focus the student on the specific area of learning.

The WWW is merely a tool, as is a chalkboard, overhead projector, or VCR. Tools don't teach. When effectively implemented they assist in the learning process. If learning on the part of the student has been helped by the use of a tool, then the tool has been used successfully. With the advent of internet technology, teachers are now faced with deciding how to make this new tool work most effectively. The internet offers unparalleled diversity for students as an interactive research tool and as a medium for publication. Its hyperlink system lends itself to a student-centred learning environment, thus soliciting a new direction for pedagogy in many content areas.

Incorporating the internet into instruction will have a tremendous impact on both the student's and the instructor's approaches to learning and teaching. The WWW presents challenges to instructors who incorporate it in their instruction. These hurdles in utilising modern resources, in addition to traditional approaches, involve the issues of time and effectiveness, instructional design, and credibility of the new resource. When working with the WWW, the instructor must first become familiar with the technology prior to assisting students in reaching their learning goals.

Like beginning the year with a new textbook, instructors need to have a general idea of what information is available and how to access it. The time needed to feel comfortable varies greatly among instructors. Once acquainted with the new medium, the instructor should choose a project already established in the curriculum and instead of relying on traditional book resources to develop it, incorporate the internet as the information resource.

By viewing the internet as a way to enhance an already developed curricular goal, the instructor decreases development time. For instructors who teach current events, accessing periodicals online in all languages can keep students updated on world events from the viewpoint of countries other than their own. As students become more comfortable, they can gather more information quickly. Beginning with a search engine, students should look for information on their topic. In order to allow for this partially structured approach, the instructor must be flexible and open to student discovery. Students are likely to find sites that even the instructor never knew existed.

In the meantime, students will learn how to work with the internet software as they develop their research skills. Some guidance with respect to linking to related documents, going to specific locations if students have an internet address, and narrowing or broadening a search to be most useful will make the job much less time consuming and intimidating. But rather than teaching the technology itself, instructors should focus on guiding students in exploring the subject matter through the utilisation of technology.

For instructors who are accustomed to a more controlled environment, one solution is to begin students at a particular location on the WWW that offers links to other related sites. Instructors should consider having a backup plan just in case they don't find what they had anticipated. In addition, instructors should be aware that when all students are accessing the same location at the same time, students may encounter difficulty downloading that page due to too much traffic. For this reason, it is recommended to move away from the more structured lesson and allow for the flexibility offered by search engines.

The WWW, on the other hand, is much more casual. Anyone can learn basic HTML scripting and can publish their thoughts on the WWW. For this reason, students need to look beyond the information they have gathered and consider the author and source. They need to decide if the source is credible enough to use the information and to defend their decision. They also develop life skills of investigation and discrimination of sources. Since the WWW is not a censored medium and permits all ideas and opinions to be broadcast worldwide, it becomes the students' responsibility to decide what is supportable evidence and what is exploitation.

Web-based communication for teaching and learning has been popularised by the constructivist-learning paradigm, which is based on collaborative learning principles.

E Mail

E mail is an inherently low-performance technology because it has only one function—to communicate. Issues of access, operability, resource distribution, and many of the design for learning indicators do not apply. However, e mail gives schools access to rich learning experiences—such as communicating with a tutor or mentor—and collaborative work. To some extent, e-mail does let students interact and explore, but some of these interactions and explorations are more powerful than others.

For example, although using e-mail to write to pen pals in another state may provide some interesting—and perhaps even some powerful—learning experiences, these are episodic and unplanned events. For more sustained challenges, students could use the same e-mail system to explore deeply complex cultural and linguistic issues or solve problems with distant peers over a period of time; teachers could communicate with practicing professionals and community members; and both students and teachers could conduct collaborative projects.

Users send and receive email text messages asynchronously through a programme installed on the user's computer, which sends and receives information through an email server provided by the user's Internet Service Provider

(ISP) or office network. However, web-based email (like Hotmail or Yahoo Mail) allows users to access their account from any computer with an internet connection. A user can send emails to multiple recipients simultaneously, and can attach files (word-processed documents, spreadsheets, images) to each message. This facilitates collaborative group learning at a distance, but puts the onus on the learner to initiate or maintain contact.

Mailing Lists

Mailing lists are many-to-many communication channels on the internet, managed using specialised software such as Listserv, Majordomo, and Listproc. People email instructions to join or leave a list to the computer running the service. Lists can be moderated or unmoderated, and can be used to collaboratively discuss and debate education or training issues within learning communities. However, too large a group can hinder rather than help the learning process.

Internet Discussion Board Systems

Internet discussion board systems such as WebBoard, Yahoogroups or Smartgroups are similar to mailing lists, with the additional feature of everyone's messages being available on the WWW as a series of discussions. Messages are displayed online as they are received or as appended replies to the original message, allowing simultaneous coverage of many topics.

Chat

Internet Relay Chat (IRC) is the standard for synchronous, multi-person, text-based chat. Most IRC applications (such as MSN Messenger, ICQ or Yahoo Messenger) are independent of the WWW, but can also be launched from a web page. The software keeps track from a central server of when you, and a list of people you specify, are online. You can text-chat or voice chat one-to-one, or in a conference. Some systems have an electronic whiteboard on which a teacher may "write" information viewable by all online chat participants, simulating a classroom situation. However, synchronous text or voice chat can create organisational problems – especially in globally offered web courses, where there are time zone issues.

MUDs, MOOs, WOOs and IRC

Multi-User Dimension (MUDs) and MUD Object Oriented (MOOS) are multi-user text-based virtual realities accessible via the internet. MUDs evolved from multi-user interactive role-playing games on the internet. The possibilities such a tool offers for education have not been ignored. The MOO variant in particular has proved highly popular for educational purposes, since it includes a powerful built-in programming language that can be used to create entirely new objects, extending the MOO virtual-world.

This ability to create objects and extend the "virtual community" is not just limited to the MOO's original creators. Indeed, the ability of users to construct new objects is arguably as important as the ability to perform group communication, a point which some educators have not always grasped. Some of the central properties of MUDs and MOOs that make them different from other kinds of Virtual Realities:

i) MUDs do not employ fancy graphics or special position-sensing hardware but rely entirely on plain, unformatted text to communicate with the users

ii) MUDs are extensible from within; MUD users can add new rooms and objects to the database and give those objects unique virtual behaviour, using an embedded programming language.

iii) MUDs generally have many users connected at the same time. All of these users are browsing and manipulating the same database and can encounter both the other users and their newly-created objects. MUD users can also communicate with each other directly, in real time, usually by typing messages that are seen by all other users in the same room.

The simplicity with which users can describe themselves and the objects they create is one of the great strengths of MUDs. A richly detailed environment can be described with a few lines of text. In order to produce an acceptable graphical representation of the same environment, much greater effort would have to be applied by the user.

There are a number of different ways in which web technologies can be combined with that of MOOs to provide a useful educational environment. One of the main arguments for using MUDs/MOOs in an educational environment is the opportunity they offer for multi-participant synchronous communication over the internet. Whilst this is also possible using IRC (Internet Relay Chat) and other synchronous protocols, MOOs also provide a sense of virtual space that mimics the real world. This metaphorical sense of 'being somewhere' serves a number of useful purposes.

The practice of anonymity in MOOs has other interesting consequences. In a MOO, someone is only 'known by what they explicitly project and are not 'locked into' any factors beyond their easy control'. Thus factors such as race, personal appearance, disability and gender need not be revealed, reducing the possibilities of prejudiced assumptions about a person and restraining physical factors. This may be one of the reasons why students who are normally quiet and non-participators in a real world classroom often become much more active in a MOO class.

As well as providing a sense of space and identity, MOOs have another major advantage over other forms of synchronous communication—the capability for users to construct objects and extend the MOO. This capacity gives MOOs not just a shared context, but also the opportunity for shared activity. This can be contrasted with, for example, browsing the web, which tends to be a much more passive activity.

For teaching purposes, some disciplines are better suited then others to the textual environment of MOOs. It is recognised that for certain subjects a more graphical approach is required (such as for some of the sciences), but for many others the ease with which complex virtual worlds can be created is a powerful capability. The nature of MOO communication makes them particularly suited for collaborative work, for example collaborative writing, or joint discussion of a literary text.

The worldwide nature of the synchronous communication possible in MOOs is also particularly suited to language learning, as there can be direct and instantaneous interaction with native speakers from different countries. Indeed, there are a number of MOOs dedicated to language learning. MOOs provide more of a total environment than, for example, email discussion lists, but this is not to say they have to be isolated from other means of online communication or real world classes.

A MOO can be thought of as just another tool in the educators tool box; it need not be a replacement for existing teaching methods, but can be considered an enhancement to them. Even if a course is to be totally online (as in distance learning, for example) some aspects of the teaching process are simply not that appropriate for use in a MOO reference materials, particularly, may be more appropriate on the web.

Computer-Aided Assessment (CAA)

Since the early seventies, computer-aided assessment (CAA) has been on the brink of revolutionising education. CAA has changed the student teacher relationship, but, unlike the direct contact of an email list or a MUD/MOO environment, this is in terms of objective performance measurement. There exist many different CAA packages, from freeware and shareware to expensive and sophisticated systems. If CAA is to be used in the formal assessment process the implementation strategy must be carefully thought out.

Instructional Management Systems (IMS)

Instructional Management Systems (IMS) is a project which developed in the United States aimed at standardising information about courseware. IMS attempts to address the problems of the perceived lack of open standards in courseware or learning materials and the systems needed to deliver these. It looks at:

i) Standards for describing learning resources
ii) Communication protocols between learning resources
iii) Accreditation (possibly financial) for the subsequent use of learning resources
iv) Systems to manage the overarching delivery and handling of learning resources

The original specifications document for IMS is filled with aims and objectives that will be strongly welcomed by most academics. It aims to produce an 'open architecture for learning' enabling learners to 'pick content from a myriad of sources available'. In other words, if IMS can deliver a satisfactory way of describing, evaluating, and sharing courseware (inter)nationally then students will be able to create their own learning processes on demand.

To anyone involved the use of online teaching the potential of IMS should be welcomed, but the practicalities of its implementation are slightly worrying. On a conceptual issue the aim to increase the lifespan of learning resources will not necessarily by standardising the metadata linked to it, but rather by standardising the creation of the resource itself. Reading through the original IMS specifications one also has to question whether all learning can be modularised to the extent it suggests. The notion that widespread use of learning materials has been held back by 'the lack of a commonly accepted specification' is uncertain.

References

Armitage, S, and Steeples, C., "Guidelines for Using Computer Conferencing in Teaching", *BT CMC in HE Newsletter*, Issue 4,1996.

Collins, M. et al., *Computer-Mediated Communication and the Online Classroom*, New Jersey, 1994.

Collis, B. et al., "Web Environments for Group-Based Project Work in Higher Education", *International Journal of Educational Telecommunications,AACE* 3.2 1997.

Crook, C., *Computers and the Collaborative Experience of Learning,* London, Routledge, 1994.

Dede, C., "Emerging technologies and distributed learning", *American Journal of Distance Education* 10, 2, 4-36, 1996.

Dillenbourg, P., et al. "Mediating the Mechanisms Which Make Collaborative Learning Sometimes Effective", *International Journal of Educational Telecommunications, AACE* 1.2, pp. 131-146, 1995.

Dubrovsky, V.J. et al, 'The Equalisation Phenomenon: Status Effects in Computer-Mediated and Face-to-Face Decision Making Groups", *Human Computer Interaction* 6, 1991.

Gibbs, G., Pollard, N., Farrell, J., *Institutional Support for Resource Based Learning*, Oxford Centre for Staff Development, 1994.

Harasim, L. et al., *Learning Networks: A Field Guide to Teaching and Learning Online,* Cambridge, MA, 1995.

Jonassen, D.H., *Computers in the Classroom: Mindtools for Critical Thinking,* Englewood Cliffs, NJ, 1996.

Jones, P., Jacobs, G., and Brown, S., "Learning Stylers and CAL Design: A Model for the Future", *Active Learning,* December 1997.

Kurland, N. D., *Computer Communication: A New Tool for Distance Education*, Heerlen & Assen/Maastricht, 1986.

Lloyd, P. *Groupware in 21st Century: Computer Supported Co-operative Working Towards the Millennium,* Adamantine Press, 1994.

McConnell, D., *Implementing Computer Supported Co-operative Learning,* London, 1994.

Oliver, M., and Conole, G. "Evaluating Communication and Information Technologies: A Tookit for Practitioners", *Active Learning,* July, 1998.

O'Malley, C. ed., *Computer Supported Collaborative Learning,* Berlin, 1994.

Rapaport, M., *Computer Mediated Communications,* New York, 1991.

Steeples, C., et al, *Technological Support for Teaching and Learning: Computer-Mediated Communications in Higher Education,* Oxford, 1996.

Wells, R., "Computer-Mediated Communication for Distance Education: An International Review of Design, Teaching and Institutional Issues", *ACSDE Research Monograph,* No.6, Pennsylvania State University, 1993.

Weiser, M., "The computer for the 21st century", *Scientific American* 265, 3, September, 1991.

6

Pedagogy of Online Teaching and Learning

Technology can be a connection that enhances learning: the connection between student and knowledge, between student and student, between student and teacher, between student and society, and so forth. Online pedagogical approaches include considering the length of time of each course activity, how to assess student learning, and how to assure academic integrity in students' learning. Special consideration to the online environment, however, are found in issues surrounding resources and logistics: in planning online testing.

Creating and designing a curriculum that encourages students to work together redefines 'cheating' as necessary 'collaboration,' surprisingly similar to work processes common to working adults. Classroom interaction is one of the most difficult challenges presented in the online learning environment. A curriculum design that relies on collaborative work also helps students to interact with one another. In some classes, assigning 'roles' to the student groups can help students move toward successful project completion. In short, utilising the pedagogy of solid group work should be enabled with online course tools. For example, chat rooms may be best for synchronous communication or for holding office hours, but a threaded discussion may be most suited for developing indepth, thoughtful student responses.

Course management tools such as WebCT provide spaces for both, and also provide space for private group work. Let students explore their ideas privately and present them publicly. It is this type of community building that helps students feel free to develop and articulate their own ideas. Let students get in the habit of using the tools for communication. These different communication tools also provide different modalities for students' learning styles.

To address the multiple learning styles in any classroom, the principles of sound pedagogy are again at the forefront. The best option is to design a variety of learning activities to address different learning styles. Course design of this nature can help students expand their learning style experiences, reinforcing their strengths and also bolstering their weaknesses. Comfort using technology is an issue separate from learning style, but will affect learning, and making sure all students are comfortable is of special concern for the diverse backgrounds common in distance education courses. Time on computer is a very important predictor of student comfort with technology.

Adult learners may need more technology orientation, so a teacher's awareness of the students' skill levels becomes very important in successful online learning. And, finally, given the multiple audiences that online learning environments may serve, remember to pay attention to special needs of adult learners. There is a generational relationship to technology. Some adult learners may not explore freely. They may be less likely to just 'go looking' on the website; they are not as apt to undertake trial-and-error as are younger audiences.

Dimensions of Online Pedagogy

Organisational change is more or less connected with change in teaching and learning. There are three dimensions in the field of online pedagogy:

i) Pedagogical principles
ii) Pedagogical functions
iii) Pedagogical variables

Pedagogical Principles

The approach of the pedagogical principles outlines on a macro-level the general trends that can be observed in the field of online pedagogy with respect to the integration of ICT into higher education and the realisation of virtual learning environments. The current online pedagogy is following up the globally desirable trend of a "shift from teaching to learning". Simultaneously the online pedagogy takes on a key position in the fundamental institutional change of the higher education sector.

The ICT changes in an increasing degree the roles and relationships of learners and teachers by interfering and changing their interactions. The student-centred approach can be seen as the common pedagogical frame for the cooperation. This approach is based on the deepened understanding of student's learning. In a mainly divided constructivist perspective the student's learning is seen rather as an active, individual and sociocultural process that is dealing with the construction of cognition and competences.

The students create in the process their own structure of knowledge of the studied discipline and they develop acting opportunities that enable them to treat knowledge in a competent manner. In the context of online pedagogy the teaching aspires to support the students in this process.

In the student-centred approach the emphasis is moving from the traditional instructional-centred teaching towards the support of learning. The construction of learning environments and learning advice is evolving as one central task of the teachers. In the setting of pedagogical interaction respective communication the teachers are less occupied with the procurement of learning material. In fact the learning material is integrated within the content management in a pedagogical design and is mainly available as virtual information in the net.

The students acquire an active role in above-described learning arrangements. To be able to fulfil this role, they do not only have to cope with the added responsibility for their learning, but also they have to dispose of suitable learning strategies. This applies to the cognitive exposure with knowledge (organisation, elaboration, critical examination and retrieval) as well as to the meta-cognitive strategies of planning, controlling and regulating the own learning processes and also the application of internal motivational and external supportive resources. In particular in relation to the knowledge management the virtual environment poses increased requirements (to the learners). But even apart from this facet the learning strategies within ICT-conditions face particular molding neccesities reacting to the special characteristics of virtual learning environments.

The objective of online pedagogy is to place a adequate support at the disposal. Thus in the area of learning strategies the so-called deep approach is favoured. The students can only adopt responsibility for their own learning process, if they are in the position to organise and steer their learning process theirselves. They can only then cope with this demand if they are able to use the prepared learning environment accordingly to their individual learning prerequisites or to adapt the environment accordingly to their needs (self-organised) and to make independent decisions regarding their learning ways (self-directed).

Learning opens up a social dimension in which evolve social competencies to act. These competencies are essential for scientific work and teamwork. In media-enabled placement the interactive and collaborative learning faces particular demands, whose handling needs special competences. In the long run cooperative and collaborative learning may lead to develop learning communities.

The global structure of the world wide web not only enables, but even demands to realise interactive and collaborative learning in an international range. At the same time international communication implies and fosters language competences. That includes not only the communicative abilities. In addition international communication is as well a tool for understanding as also an instrument to access new horizons of understanding, in which the personal knowledge can be integrated into the globalised scientific culture and leds to a better multicultural understanding.

The online pedagogy disposes of an abundant repertoire of simulative methods, which enable the observation and manipulation of a multitude of correlations, that keep hidden in real time and real environments. The disadvantages of inadequate real encounters stands *vis-à-vis* to the advantages of an intensive reflection with pedagogical reconstructions. The different principles can be more or less combined to characterise teaching and learning in the online mode.

Pedagogical Functions

Pedagogical functions are organised within the perspective of educational beliefs around topics like content, process and media-based scientific learning and studying. The world of technological and media-based rooms is seen as a variable design of these technological options and embedded in a context of configured knowledge management, cognition and reflection, communication and action.

Indeed this procedure demands a solid infrastructural supply with plurality of technique and media. Solitary and system-embedded, excellent solutions are also urgently needed. This demands a pedagogy of open scenarios and adequate media-based blended-learning environments, in which courses of present and net-based teaching and learning in higher education coexist and add to each other.

Pedagogical action aims at interrelating teaching and learning. On the one hand teaching in this sense serves the purpose to enable respective facilitate learning. If it is not just the case of individual learning—which are common in learning contexts of higher education—but the interaction within a learning group and with a teachers is meant, the teaching defines the modus of interaction, in so far as the interaction takes place within the learning process.

In this sense facilitation and moderation constitute basic pedagogical functions that have to be realised in online teaching respective blended learning exactly like in a face-to-face situation. The peculiarity in online teaching respective blended learning is the mediation of these functions by means of ICT. The whole range of pedagogical options for arranging face-to-face courses has to be transferred into ICT—environments and to be equipped with new of norms of communication adequate for the media.

ICT environments offer particular media-based qualities that are singular and specific compared to other types of media. They change the handling of knowledge and information, the representation, the perception, the communication and the production of knowledge. In contexts of teaching and learning this development is observed as enrichness of heurisics by means of embroadened techniques of retrieval, programme-based solutions for presentation and visualisation, socio-technical systems of knowledge management or collaboration, modelling virtualisation.

Cognitive tools add to and enhance the pedagogical perspectives on the subject of teaching and learning. The diversity of cognitive tools can be arranged in levels of complexity. Tools that enable one's own achievements of construction in the net possess already a more complex structure like, e.g., tools for authoring or modelling of presentations. Also in reference to ICT competencies different levels of complexity can be differed.

These cognitive tools and technical competencies are arranged preliminary to the pedagogical competencies relating to ICT. In a deeper sense they have to be integrated into the pedagogical strategies. These pedagogical strategies range from moderation respective guidance of learning and work processes and the preparation of course concepts like tutorials to pedagogical meta-models. The pedagogical meta-modelling offers tools for the orientation and the arrangement of pedagogical designs, e.g., situated learning, problem-based learning, case-oriented studies and so on.

Learning strategies achieve a special importance in ICT environments. They are the answers to questions regarding motivation, socialisation, habitus, cognitive and meta-cognitive competences, volitional competence, curiosity and waywardness. Currently ICT favours the visual sense and curtails the human perception with the sensual reduced interface design. Hence elaborate designed interfaces try to reconstruct the perceivable of the interface. The far reaching consequences of this development result in the artificial reintroduction of dimensions of perception.

If learning strategies are not appropriately respected within the face-to face classes, the new environments offer the chance of an integral reconstruction of the learning actions. In addition the problem shows a new facet on the level of ICT environments. Learn media, cognitive tools and simulation media tend to insribe curricula, pedagogies and strategies of learning into the programs of ICT. Thus they become implicit qualities of the programs. In contrast it is important to explicitly form the curricula, pedagogy and learning competence and to make them flexible for arrangement and perceivable within the media.

As a consequence the democratic legitimation of the construction process of media, the process of reconstuction in the context of teaching and learning and the arrangement in permanence result as new tasks. The assessment in ICT environment serves mainly two purposes: on the one hand the institutional and administrative steering, control and evaluation qualification processes and on the other hand the steering and evaluation of teaching and learning processes. Regarding the current circumstances it can be observed the extension of the technical and media infrastructure for institutional and administrative tasks, in particular as a consequence of micro-structured modularisation and international competition.

From the perspective of pedagogical functionality the steering and evaluation of teaching and learning processes and the involved actors are at least of the same, if not of higher importance. There is a reconstruction of the assessment as a steering instrument for the environment of teaching and learning needed.

In this context a set of instruments is moving into the focus such as self-observation, self-description, differentiated and scaled processes of feedback and tracking of activities, the realisation of minutes and portfolios, symmetric feedback of students regarding feedback, the steering of learning processes and finally motivating assessments of teachers. They are integral part of a scientific qualification process based primarily on self-directed and self-organised processes, that in the sense of a research-based study and learning-based research is edging closer to academic qualification and initiation to the premise of science. As universal recording machines ICT media are good instruments of assessment. But nonetheless they include a whole range of problems regarding the security of data and privacy. Moreover the attention should focus on program-embedded solutions that support the self-steering with respect to the privacy, room for options and choices, social awareness and distinctive ideas.

The most important and comprehensive innovation supported by hypermedia-environments are collaborative learning scenarios. There is a big chance for changing traditional roles and making and taking new roles. Patterns of behaviour can be changed and new patterns should be set up, that refer to a symmetric teaching and learning behaviour. A new relationship between learners makes them partners first of all and allow support for learning strategies, which are best described by coaching strategies and coaching scenarios. Changing perspectives, changing characters and social roles allow to construct a stage for multiperspective learning scenarios.

Pedagogical Variables

Teaching and learning in virtual learning environments is restricted by the constraints that are incorporated within the nature of technology itself. The scope of variation for arranging education in technology-based environments is limited by the borderlines the technology imposes on the different actors as well as on the learning material. In this sense pedagogical variables constitute the various small options that adding to a whole determine the interior of a virtual classroom, the design of the digital content and consequently the course for action of the teachers and learners working in a virtual environment.

The role of technology in universities can be seen as an agent of structural innovation and change. The current innovation in the higher education sector is caused by a variety of different factors. Online pedagogy the integration of new technologies into the teaching and learning processes of the universities is clearly the most important aspect. The pedagogical variables that account for the design of technological learning scenarios and digital platforms are without doubt situated on the borderline between online pedagogy and the organisation of higher education institutions.

It is highly reasonable that the pedagogical variables in form of concepts and ideal learning scenarios should influence the institutional policy related to the integration of eLearning into the institution. But the pedagogical variables should regulate also within the technological boundaries the design of virtual classrooms. Additional tasks of the online pedagogy include the assessment of content management systems with regard to usability aspects, the organisation of digital information in virtual learning environments and the evaluation of administration tools for the tutoring staff.

The digitalisation of the knowledge in higher education represents a second major area of technologically induced innovation in the universities. The new form of digital knowledge representation and availability induces new ways of information retrieval by the students and as a consequence demands new forms of information supply by the faculty staff. The traditional way of classroom teaching meets with additional information and discussion channels in virtual workspaces.

Online pedagogy is in charge to develop guidelines for the design of digital content and the interoperability of digital courses in different learning platforms. Online pedagogy offers a set of variables that can act as guidelines for the design of such online courses and refer to every single stage in the production process. The pedagogical approach can help you to structure the existing learning material by arranging learning sequences for your digital content.

The innovative powers of the new technologies pave the way for the construction of alternative paths to information sources for teachers and students alike. The faculty staff has to adapt to the new role of the lecturer, that is, to move from the traditional instruction style to a position where he tutors and facilitates the more independent, self-directed learning processes of the students. Online pedagogy needs to offer additional models for the realisation of this shift in teaching in higher education.

The pedagogy offers a wide range of methods for the traditional way of learning in classrooms. These methods have been proved for a long time and quite some of their elements can be transferred and applied as pedagogical variables for teaching in the virtual classroom. Among these variables that define the interior of virtual learning environment approaches as:

i) to attend to human factors/ make participants visible.
ii) to create small classes with qualified tutor.
iii) to offer prompt response.
iv) to hold pre-class gathering.
v) to publish a comprehensive syllabus.
vii) to prepare learners to participate.
viii) to manage collaboration activities/ maintain collaborative channels.
ix) to conduct live events.
x) to follow up after event.
xi) to stay in touch after the class.
xii) to monitor learning.

Learning depends in a high degree from the internal motivation of the learner. As the shift from teaching to learning implies that the learner will actively have to follow his or her course of studies, we should try to integrate some features that are based on interaction. Technology-based activities serve the main objectives to activate learning in the virtual classroom. It is useful in this stage of the process to define the components of learning activities and to use the technology in order to realise common learning activities such as:

a) webcast
b) presentation sequences
c) drill and practice

d) scavenger hunt
e) guided research
f) guided analysis
g) team design
h) brainstorming

Technology-enhanced activities are a learning method that has to be treated with care, because things can always go wrong in technology. The technology-based innovation of the higher education systems affects the way students organise their learning. The digitalisation of information leads to completely new forms of knowledge representation within universities. The traditional classroom system limited the access to relevant information for the students to printed documents and the lecture and discussion that evolved in the courses.

The digital representation of knowledge adds new gateways for the students to the relevant documents they need for their learning. In respect to the learners the online pedagogy is engaged to develop concepts for the various situations in which the students are confronted with elements of virtual learning environments. This means that the learner should be able to have access to all the necessary information within the eLearning environment.

The new technologies cause a merger process of the different kind of services that a university offers to them. The university administration has to take care that the integration of eLearning offers a consistent picture of the merging of different services in virtual universities such as:

a) paying the university fees
b) offering student services
c) giving academic assistance
d) generating general discipline and course information
e) assisting enrolment in the courses

Learning communities are enriching the learning process in virtual learning environments and can serve as a good base for the students to exchange ideas and find collaborative solutions for certain tasks. But a vivid learning community depends on a high level of support from the teachers to build up and promote collaboration between the learners. The internet offers specific collaboration tools that are useful for the communication in learning communities such as:

a) email
b) discussion groups
c) chat
d) whiteboard
e) screen sharing
f) response pads
g) audioconferencing
h) videoconferencing

Pedagogical changes in Online Instruction

An occuring pedagogical changes make the online teaching/ learning experience a positive one. There are seven principles for good teaching practice that apply to both traditional in-class instruction and online instruction. The principles can serve as a guide as materials and learning exercises are developed. The principles are:

i) encourage contact between students and faculty,
ii) develop reciprocity and cooperation among students,
iii) encourage active learning,
iv) give prompt feedback, emphasise time on task,
v) communicate high expectations, and
vi) and respect diverse talents and ways of learning.

Initial benefits to online learning were believed to be cost effectiveness access to new learners and unable to attend traditional classes. It is generally agreed that the initial cost associated with developing an online course is much higher than the sustained cost of teaching the course once it is developed but that cost effectiveness benefits are not immediate. It is obvious that the flexibility of scheduling available with online learning enables many nontraditional students to acquire an education.

Furthermore, the use of online information for teaching provides more immediacy than traditional textbooks. While there are truly a number of advantages to online teaching and learning, there are new challenges as well.

i) class size may be smaller than a traditional course due to the volume of online communication that must be processed by the instructor.
ii) computing skills are a prerequisite to an online course, not a by-product of it.
iii) technical limitations and issues might introduce problems to be overcome.
iv) communications (chat and discussions) can be unfocused unless the instructor exercises a strong guiding influence on the conversation with prompts, cues, and suggestions.
v) the demographics of students in online courses and in traditional courses is usually different.

There are a number of technologies that can be used for online instruction. A number of these technologies are used to facilitate communication among students and with the instructor. Knowing some characteristics of the tools enables an instructor to adopt the best tool for his or her purpose. WebCT and MIX both provide several useful communication tools that can be used to enhance your course. Additionally there are a number of free and commercial applications that can be used for course-based communications. These tools are both synchronous (chat and instant messages) and asynchronous (course-based email and bulletin board/ discussions).

Most aynchronous communication tools are one-to-many approaches involving a user (e.g., instructor) posting a message and responses from other users being posted at a later time (bulletin board, discussion, listserv). That is, a single person's message is read by multiple other people engaging in this activity at different times. Although often overlooked because it is used so commonly, asynchronous communication can also be one-to-one (Email). Inherently, one-to-many and one-to-one asynchronous communication allows the learner more time to reflect on the topic at hand before sending or posting a message. Additionally, with one-to-many communications the effect of audience typically generates more effort in message composition.

Many learners are accustomed to using chat for recreational purposes which is often very informal and quickly composed without reflection. Effectively adopting chat for academic purposes requires structure and effective moderation of the discussion. As a synchronous tool, chat is usually one-to-many and involves all participants being online simultaneously and often has them interacting at the same time. Without time for reflection, some instructors have found it effective to prepare students in advance with specific questions or content for them to mull over before engaging in dialogue.

As a one-to-one tool, many instructors are finding instant messaging to be an effective tool for conducting virtual office hours and for providing more responsiveness to student requests. There are a number of other technologies used for online learning that go beyond communication tools. Most web-based course management solutions offer quizzes, course information, calendars, and a number of other features.

References

Catherine M, Gynn, Ph.D., "The Pedagogy of Technology Enhanced Learning Environments".

Chickering, A.W., and Gamson, Z.F., "Applying the Seven Principles for Good Practice in Undergraduate Education, Fall 1991", San Francisco: Jossey-Bass Inc., *New Directions for Teaching and Learning*, 1991

Dabbah, N., *Using a web-based course management tool to support face-to-face instruction*, 25 February 2002.

Heiner, Matthias, Schneckenberg, Dirk and Wildt, Johannes, "Online Pedagogy— Innovative Teaching and Learning Strategies in ICT-Environments" Background paper of the cevu workgroup Online Pedagogym 2001.

Klemm, W., *Eight Ways to get students more involved in online conferences*, 21 August 2001.

7

Quality in Teaching and Learning

The extraordinary growth of technology-mediated distance learning in higher education has prompted several different organisations to develop principles, guidelines, or benchmarks to ensure quality distance education. The quality assurance benchmarks promoted by these organisations are designed to apply to a wide variety of institutional contexts and consist of fairly broad statements.

Virtually all of the strategies include such topics as course development, faculty training, student services, learning resources, infrastructure, and outcomes assessment. Internet-based distance education is quickly becoming the predominant technology in distance education, which is not surprising given the accelerating power of personal computers, increasing telecommunications bandwidth capabilities, and state-of-the-art software development and delivery.

Internet's profound influence on distance education is also important to point out that a growing number of faculty are using the internet to complement traditional classroom-based courses. For instance, it is not uncommon for course syllabi to be placed on the web. Faculty also are using cyberspace to provide access to threaded discussions, group activities, and quizzes for their on-campus students. Internet-based distance education allows the teaching/learning process to occur "at any time and any place." The ability to provide asynchronous interactive learning activities has become the signature characteristic of this technology, setting it apart from most of the other technologies.

Internet-based instruction also allows the teacher and learner to communicate over any distance to any place; it alters the concept of time. Generally, students can participate in a course at any time of day or night they choose. Due to these features, internet-based distance education is, in many ways, fundamentally different from traditional classroom-based education. Among other things, it is this distinctly different concept of time that engenders concern and scepticism from many in the higher education community.

The beauty of the web is that it provides an entirely new context for teaching and learning. It removes the physical and time constraints for instructors as well as learners. How can a teaching/learning process that deviates so markedly from what has been practiced for hundreds of years embody quality education? This question has been addressed in many ways by the range of benchmarks developed by a variety of organisations concerned about quality distance education.

Qualities of Online Learning

Computer and internet use has grown tremendously in recent years in households and workplaces. The attraction of computer-based and internet-delivered education and training is therefore not surprising. Many people have access to the necessary hardware required either at work or at home, and individual households are hooking up to the internet in ever-increasing numbers.

Online learning is often combined with other approaches, making it difficult to isolate and measure. In fact, pure online learning would rarely be the mode of first choice for students and would generally only be used when other approaches are not readily available. Students prefer hybrid approaches which mix modes of delivery, resources and technologies to achieve maximum flexibility and interaction withboth teaching staff and their fellow students. In this way the learning processes accommodate a range of preferred learning styles. Online technologies are used to facilitate contact and communication between staff and students and between the students themselves. They are also used to introduce an element of face-to-face communication or to improve interaction where classroom delivery is impossible or difficult. Good communication is one of the key features students look for in a teaching program. Calculating the precise nature and amount of online learning actually occurring was difficult.

What researchers were able to measure probably only represents a relatively small proportion of the actual online delivery taking place across the vocational education and training (VET) sector. Improved information is needed on the full range of delivery approaches being used at provider level. Online delivery to students based off-campus may appear, on the surface, to be a low-cost option when compared with traditional distance education delivery by correspondence. However, when compared with traditional modes of distance delivery, it appeared to be more costly because of the extra support learners required or demanded.

Some studies shows that there needs to be a move away from learner-content interaction and towards learner-instructor and learner-learner interaction. This is not surprising as most students emphasise the importance of the social and networking aspects of learning. There are three most important quality features for students (in order) are:

i) *Flexibility*: Flexibility to be able to work at the time, place and pace that the student chooses; accessibility, convenience, freedom and blending delivery approaches to provide a variety of learning outcomes and pathways.

ii) *Responsive teachers*: Teachers who are motivators and helpers and respond promptly, thoughtfully, comprehensively and in an informed way to requests for help and in other contexts; who keep in regular contact by bulletins, phone, email or other means and indicate their availability; who build good relationships with students and develop trust.

iii) *Quality of materials and course design*: Materials that are fast to download, easy-to-read, uptodate, interactive, comprehensive and well-designed, with clear navigation and structures, clear directions to learners, containing ways by which students can judge their progress

Figure 1 provides a visual presentation of these key quality features and also includes a fourth important feature of online learning from the learner's perspective. This is the 'self ' feature—the individual attributes that learners require to 'succeed' online.

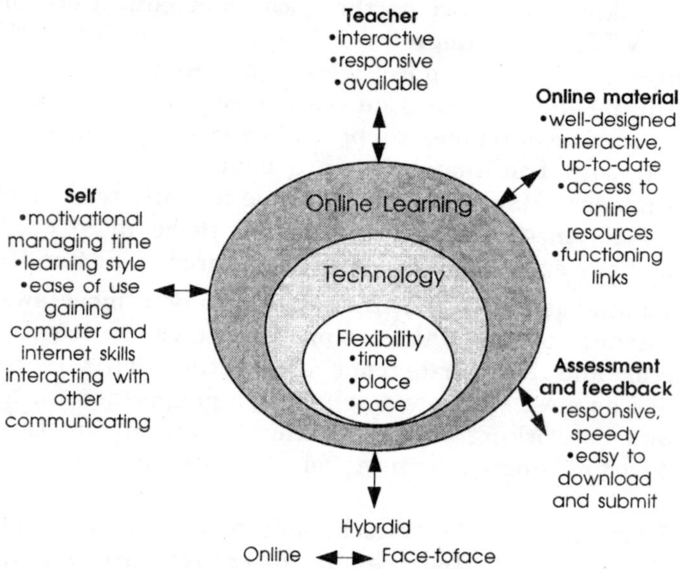

Figure 1. Factors for high-quality online learning

Possessing these attributes will influence considerably the quality and effectiveness of their online learning experience. The key features of a quality online learning experience that were identified by teachers are very similar to those identified by students, but with an additional emphasis on student support issues and drawing attention to organisational and professional development aspects of the introduction and delivery of learning online.

The research suggests that the online environment demands that teachers develop new ways of building relationships that rely more on emails, chat rooms and other devices, which require high-level written and other communication skills. An important success factor in online learning is developing rapport with the students: knowing them, their progress and their interests intimately to help to enrich their learning experiences as much as possible. Teachers suggested that their preparation of online learning materials is no more time-consuming than the preparation of print materials. However, all agreed that teaching and managing online demands more time than does teaching an equivalent group in class, especially when the program is self-paced.

Professional development is needed in a wide range of areas to help teachers make better use of online learning and delivery. Professional development needs were recognised in relation to reflecting on pedagogical issues, using the technologies, seeing what others are doing, keeping up to date with new developments in a fast-moving field, resource development and, importantly, the development of adequate levels of written and other communication skills for the online environment.

Teachers need training in online facilitation, especially in the management of self-paced groups. Moderation of online discussion groups was an element of online teaching that was thought to need particular attention. As an example, teachers need to understand protocols that are available for online interaction in web discussion, chat and other approaches, to ensure that all those who wish to participate can do so. It was suggested that teachers who already have good management and teaching skills may find such tasks easier.

Benefits of Online Learning

Today, fifty per cent of higher education institutions currently engage in some type of online learning. Academic and professional organisations agree that using web-based learning environments can offer sound pedagogical benefits.

Web-based education tools provide many ways to increase communication between class members and faculty, including discussion boards, chats, and e-mails.

Online forums, like Blackboard's Discussion Board and Chat, provide public areas to post information. Each student can view another student's answers and learn through the exposure to different perspectives. This benefits students because they can combine new opinions with their own, and develop a solid foundation for learning.

Another benefit to using web-based communication tools is to give all students a reinforced sense of equality. Each individual has the same opportunity to "speak up" by posting messages without typical distractions such as seating arrangements, volume of student voices, and gender biases. Shy and anxious students feel more comfortable expressing ideas and backing up facts when posting online instead of speaking in a lecture room. Studies prove that online discussions provoke more confrontational and direct communication between students.

Online communication also benefits students by providing additional layer of instructor accessibility. Students in courses that are supplemented by products like Blackboard no longer have to worry if they cannot make an instructor's regular office hours, as they still have the ability to submit inquiries via e-mail at any time. This is good for the instructor too, as they can respond at his/her convenience instead of being tied to a desk or office.

Every student has a unique learning style. Some students are visual learners, some learn better when they "learn by doing." Web-based learning environments permit the instructor to build one course, yet implement a variety of resources, so students can utilise materials in whichever way works best for them. An instructor can also present these materials in many formats to accommodate different types of learning styles.

When course content and activities are provided online, students no longer need to worry about accessing course materials. Students can complete assignments during their most productive times. In traditional education, students working on group projects must coordinate schedules. In distance learning environments, this may not even be possible, forcing participants to work independently. When web-based collaborative tools are available, coordination is no longer an issue.

Learner assessments are essential in education. Tests and surveys inform the instructor whether teaching methods and course structures are successful. These assessments also determine if student progress is satisfactory. Online assessment tools provide instructors with many ways to build, distribute, and compile information quickly and easily.

Web-based testing features also have pedagogical benefits. Frequent assessment provides concept reinforcement and increases motivation. Instructors can post practice exams and end-of-chapter reviews without worrying about finding the time and resources to analyse results. Students can access these assessments at any time, privately and in the comfort of their home. Since grading is computerised, students receive immediate feedback. This may also help students who suffer from test anxiety relax and minimise embarrassment for those that do poorly.

In addition to the pedagogical benefits of online learning, there are also several time and money saving advantages. Students can save and print items as needed when provided with handouts and readings online. The direct result is a reduced institutional expense for both the cost and time associated with copying, collating, and distributing these materials. The time saving elements introduced by web-based education tools like Blackboard apply to both the instructor and the student. Students benefit because they have immediate access to course materials at any location.

ICT APPLICATIONS TO IMPROVE QUALITY EDUCATION

ICT application to the core business of education can accelerate and improve learning on a number of fronts, from basic skills; problem solving, information management, work habits, motivation, establishing life-long learning habits and concepts development. Information and communication technologies are being applied to the management of learning and to the business models of educational delivery.

ICT can make to quality in teaching, learning and evaluation through improvements in cognition, pedagogies, convergence, culture, and data. There are several levels on which ICTs can push the cognition boundaries. New media allow us to represent in rich and diverse ways. This is not simply a matter of learning styles although diverse learning styles can be supported by ICT.

ICT allows to accelerate or decelerate processes for purposes of understanding. The best cognitive understandings and practice can be captured and communicated by ICTs and applied to the task of growing minds in ways that improve the quality of learning for many, rather than few children. ICTs can give teachers access to great conceptualisers to assist them in planning and programming cognitive development. Best of all, the interactive capacity of ICTs provides more opportunities for students to engage as creators and manipulators in the learning process.

ICTs bringing together aesthetic as well as scientific considerations, allowing to overlay knowledge and meaning with skill and competence. ICTs qualitatively improve cognition by conceptualising more creatively, improving teachers' knowledge and by tailoring learning resources to meet the particular needs of a child at every stage of his or her education. It has been widely recognised that harnessing the power of modern technologies for learning purposes requires that appropriate learning strategies be developed that harmonise effectiveness in learning with the technology role. ICTs provide many opportunities to more easily use a variety of pedagogies.

As a tool, ICTs can support didactic or facilitative approaches, collaboration and interaction across time and distance, enquiry or interrogation, open or closed research, lock step or mind-map. Online technologies support and make easier constructivist approaches, just as they make behaviourist approaches easier. The capacity of ICT to deliver information or to communicate with a mass of students in quite individual ways opens up the possibility of tailoring pedagogy to the needs of a student in time and place without the limitations imposed by peer groups. This provides the opportunity for software that utilises, for example, multiple intelligence theory.

ICTs, lend themselves very readily to holistic learning, collaborative grouping, problem-oriented activities and integrated thematic units. Teachers wishing to teach in this way will be both more efficient and effective if they employ ICTs to reach their goals. The ICTs of themselves will not improve pedagogy. They will, however, support and assist teachers who shift their pedagogies to be more student-d, project-based and collaborative. Scaffolding techniques are readily supported by ICTs. Systems, principals and teacher training institutions can use ICT to drive in these directions, using it to provide the scaffolding for the teacher as the teacher does for the student.

Medical technologies are converging with educational technologies online technologies are converging with offline technologies (through, for example, the use of XML), digital technologies are interacting with media, with publishing industries, with entertainment, distribution and production industries. Such convergence has profound implications for the organisation, management and conception of education and educational delivery. Inevitably, convergence is also occurring within the curriculum, across traditional subject areas, most of which were classified in the eighteenth and nineteenth centuries.

Knowledge management, using the organising capacity of digital technology is another. Alignment is another. Multiskilling seeks to layer skills over knowledge areas, constructing a matrix that brings together, at the point of an educational outcome, both subject knowledge and discipline, with other skills or competencies. Multiskilling places high demands on teachers, who must themselves be multiskilled in order to manage the multiskilling demands of a curriculum.

Information and communication technologies play a significant part in multiskilling because they provide enabling tools to speed processes and link knowledge. Knowledge management brings search engines, thesauri, 'see also' and 'see' algorithms to link data-bases, texts, graphics,

Following are the three measures of quality teaching and learning.

i) Student interaction with faculty and other students is an essential characteristic and is facilitated through a variety of ways, including voice-mail and/or e-mail.

ii) Feedback to student assignments and questions is constructive and provided in a timely manner.

iii) Students are instructed in the proper methods of effective research, including assessment of the validity of resources.

To be fair, a number of other measures clearly relate to pedagogy, but it is also apparent that these three benchmarks derive from traditional approaches to teaching and learning and do not encompass current theories of teaching and learning such as consructivism.

References

Alexander, Shirley, "Teaching and Learning on the World Wide Web", AusWeb 97 Conference, 1997.

Barker, K., "Quality guidelines for online education and training", 12th April 2002

Brown, J., Collins, A.&Duguid, P., "Situated cognition and the culture of learning", *Educational Researcher*,18,32-42, 1989.

Dwyer, Dan, Barbieri, Kathy, Doerr, Helen, "Creating a Virtual Classroom for Interactive Education on the Web", *The Third International World Wide Web Conference*, 1995.

Golas, K., "Guidelines for designing online learning", 12th April 2002.

Herrington, Anthony, Bunker, Alison, "Quality teaching online:Putting pedagogy first" Edith Cowan University, Perth, Australia.

Herrington, A, Sparrow, H, Herrington, J., "Masters Online:Designing a university-wide curriculum development", In M.Wallace, A.Ellis, D.Newton, Eds., *Proceedings of the Moving Online Conference,* Lismore,NSW:Southern Cross University, 2000.

Herrington, J, Oliver, R., "An instructional design framework for authentic learning environments", *Educational Technology Research and Development*,48 (3), 23-48, 2000.

Wilson,B.G., Ed., "Constructivist learning environments:Case studies in instructional design", Englewood Cliffs, NJ:Educational Technology Publications, 1996.

8

Assessing Teaching Effectiveness and Learning Outcomes

The role of information and communication technologies (ICTs) in education cannot be separated from the changes of education. These changes are nonlinear and have their roots and sources in society. Looking closely at the relation of education and society from a systemic point of view, it seems that new practices will emerge as forerunners of tomorrow's education: the demands from a new society can no longer be met by the current education system.

The basic concepts of our education system are being replaced, as the challenges towards education cannot be solved anymore within the existing educational framework. Computers, especially when they are linked in networks, have the potential to change everyday classroom practice dramatically. The impact of the use of ICT in education will not be limited to the actors involved in the learning process (teachers and students), but will also change the institutional infrastructure, relations and patterns of behaviour within the education system, and even the content of education.

For a good understanding of these educational changes it is necessary to look at the transformation our society (in the industrialised countries) is undergoing. In fact, education is reacting to the emergence of the information society. Traditionally, schools provided the settings where individuals were being prepared for the industrial society. In this society the focus was on 'making things', on industrial production.

The mission of the education system is to provide balanced, personal, social, and vocational education, facilitating personal growth and development, citizenship, and providing preparation for a profession. Quality of education can be defined as the amount to which education is capable of realising these goal.

Today's education system faces the challenge to prepare individuals for the information society in which one of the most important aims is to handle information. Besides this challenge the education systemis also facing other challenges.

i) *A contribution is expected from education to the solution of social, cultural and economical problems of society:* Education can no longer stand aside from all the problems of society: isolation, ethnic integration, juvenile delinquency, non-labour, etc. There is massive evidence that the level of someone's education correlates directly to the opportunities someone has in society.

ii) *People want education to be individualised and flexible, suited to their specific needs:* Growing individualisation in and diversification of society calls for specific approaches in education. Standardised methods and classroom approaches will no longer be sufficient for individual needs.

iii) *Lifelong learning and new demands for learning:* The growing number of people that is participating in education is the main problem that has to be addressed by the educational community. The guarantee for open and equal access to education for everybody is becoming almost unaffordable under the current circumstances.

The near future provides all kinds of challenges and opportunities for the education system in our society. Managing large amounts of information, developing learning strategies to facilitate effective learning, and assuring that all citizens are proficient in assessing, selecting, and dealing with information are of critical importance. It is assumed that a shift from teacher oriented arrangements of the learning process towards more student oriented arrangements will be necessary.

Assessment Teaching Effectiveness

The modern university, as one ideological arm of the nation state, is a bureaucratic, corporate, capitalist organisation. This volatile role for the university triggers a new vocabulary: of excellence, standards, flexibility and efficiency. It is densely ironic that universities have entered a period of crisis at the very time when women, mature aged students and ethnic minorities are entering the institution. In such an environment, a national curriculum makes little sense. Instead, the link between tradition and the market has affiliated the directives of neo-conservatives with neoliberals. Both ideologies pathologise popular knowledges.

The modalities of crisis and economic rationalism are framing the current movement into internet-based teaching. The motif of 'crisis' provides an unfortunate and inappropriate push into technological innovation. Through these changes, the academy has been resilient and flexible. The shift in motifs, from the ivory tower to the real world, has downplayed and demeaned the critical function of scholars. The desire for concrete knowledge, serving pressing economic concerns, is not only promoted by conservative governments.

Cyberspace becomes the virtual library and university — and the fount of all knowledge. Such a stance decentres the place and expertise of academics. Internet-based learning is a response to consumerism and the reduction in government funding. This has been an unfortunate context for the expansion of online pedagogy. The language of computer-based systems — cost savings, efficiency, and productivity — has masked the public interest and investment in information technologies.

Roles of Teachers

The teaching skills being developed in our age include how to teach larger classes and be more entrepreneurial. The four pillars of academic life — teaching, research, administration and community service — are the postwar foundations of the current system. The rapid post-world war 'innovations' in the education, when accompanied by vocationalism and the rise of structural youth unemployment, have altered the requirements of teachers and teaching. The polarised institutional and educational priorities trigger the rhetoric of competing effectively for additional students while maintaining the same or a smaller faculty.

Technology is generally framed as a cheaper, more efficient replacement for university teachers. Investigating the cultural politics of information in this context necessitates epistemological spadework that situates teachers and teaching within the electronic classrooms. A radical reworking of teaching has taken place in the last ten years. As teachers become facilitators, and lectures transform into workshops, the notion of effective education has morphed. Good teaching practices tend to work as partnerships between teachers and students, creating student-centred learning. The teacher's role thus becomes less central, but definitely not unimportant.

Teachers, as the group responsible for curriculum, methodology and assessment, are not only "not unimportant", but absolutely critical to the reputation and success of students and universities. Internet-based learning actually increases academic workloads, because somebody needs to design the content and layout. Somebody needs to write the web pages. Somebody needs to ensure that hypertext links are uptodate. Somebody needs to create evaluative criteria. Somebody needs to administer the students' results. Therefore, student-centred learning is not only rhetoric, but also an ideological mask to deflect attention away from the power that teachers hold, and the increased workload necessary to promote web-based education.

The point of internet-based education is to relieve staff of some face-to-face teaching, so that universities become cheaper to run and more productive. Current internet teaching is not addressing these issues, but is becoming a time-consuming add-on to already full working days.

The transformation of students into consumers of knowledge and customers of the academy has major consequences for teachers. Today, the university is expected to treat its students as consumers, and so students have begun to blame their teachers for their failures. Such an attitude ignores the complex process of learning. To read, remember, understand, synthesise and interpret knowledge is frequently drudgery. To learn with effectiveness requires repetition, practice and failure. To create a cycle of disillusionment, disappointment and blame is to undermine the activity of learning and teaching. This change has been caused because knowledge has been transformed into competence. Very rarely discussed in the administrative push to online education is the high level of online withdrawal rates. Therefore, while computers are seen to promote access to education, there are substantial structural problems to address.

Internet-based education is not replacing conventional lectures and tutorials. Instead, web-based teaching is becoming one more site of writing and administration. The internet has increased the access to the instructor. While such access can be framed as beneficial to students and education broadly defined, it has emerged during the very period when research and administrative responsibilities have also increased. Some theorists question why staff lack motivation, and resist internet-based teaching . For the first time, staff must place attention on delivery management systems. In the past, staff wrote study guides, but did not have to think about how the publication was photocopied and distributed. Now, they must not only write teaching materials, but structure it within templates, keep hypertext links current, and address student queries when they cannot access the site.

While the conditions in which academics are working are changing and becoming saturated with economic imperatives, university structures are still reliant on the vocationalism and good will of scholars. There is an assumption that teachers will complete work and training for which they are not paid. Teachers have taken time away from research, marking and in-class preparation to develop a new site of knowledge.

Many university scholars have freely given time for a pedagogy that has increased their own workload. The long-term consequence of computer ubiquity is that organisations and individuals are committed to banal tasks and skills. Such activities have transformed teachers into managers of information and designers of web sites.

Administration and Management

The administration of internet-based learning is a process of negotiation and collaboration between individual academics, colleagues, and university structures.

While good teachers recognise that learning can only take place if students feel comfortable to make mistakes, the institutional framework does not encourage such an imperative. If teachers are granted a lecture theatre then they are able to ensure that the students have access to the learning environment. However this power is removed from teachers in the desire for flexibility and facilitation.

Teachers are responsible for learning, but have no ability to guarantee student access. If a university server is down, if the WebCT structure has disenabled guest account creation, then students cannot enter sites, and the instructor becomes responsible for a situation over which they can do little except write placating e mails. HTML offers enormous potential for the development of innovative educational architecture. The simple format for both representing and linking documents is an outstanding opportunity to create new types of referencing, writing and reading. The repercussions of hypertext for those who both teach and assess the work of others is also far reaching.

There is the capacity for immediate questioning and feedback on work. Immediate feedback is also possible through written essays, but a one/two-week turnaround is the standard. The potential of hypertext raises the possibility of the moment an essay arrives, it can be marked — either through the tracking function in Microsoft Word, or via Notepad. Invariably, this "immediate feedback" does not result.

The managerial makeover of the contemporary university has resulted in a re-evaluation of the curriculum. In evaluating the virtual curriculum, questions should be raised about both teacher education and professional development. The managerialism of the current university system has meant that internet-based pedagogy has been focused on design issues, rather than rationale, intentions or applications.

The laissez faire attitude to teacher training has relied on 'gifted amateurs,' rather than structural change, initiating internet-based education. Too often however, the major managerial decisions promote the desire for flexible learning. Particular instructors are protecting their area, by streamlining units and making their courses 'economically viable.'

Pedagogical or political rationales were irrelevant to the web-based transfer of literature. With such a tiny enrolment, online education was a desperate act to keep the course viable.

The polarised impact of information technology within the university can be attributed to a lack of training in the mid-to late 1990s. While most institutions made internet training "available", they did not reduce the workload so that staff could take up this opportunity. That early absence has resulted in a lack of critical reflexivity and familiarity on reading and writing for the web, and an overemphasis on the technology "itself". While technology continues to "advance", it will not be used appropriately unless crafted alongside pedagogy.

Flexibility and Excellence

The two motifs of the university, flexibility and excellence, have also marked internet studies and internet-based instruction. A student questionnaire, probing the rationale for web-based teaching, hinted at the pressures confronting academics to "be flexible". The far-reaching demands of students in this new environment perhaps foreshadow the future of university education.

These are not self-regulated learners. These student responses are not strong advocates for the benefits of the internet for learning, teaching or the credibility of a university. The desire for students to contact staff whenever and however they desire would be unexpected in most business environments. Such desires from students appear not only ungracious, but are treating academic staff like a customer service agency.

Within the increased managerial load on academics, there will be less hours in the day when students can see teachers or have their calls answered. Even though materials have been put online, and the potential of asynchronous communication mobilised, students want e mails to be answered quickly. Similarly staff are to be available by e mail and phone and fax and personally. Therefore, online education has actually created a new problem, which will fragment the workplace further, and must make an academic‘s workday less efficient.

Most online students describe flexibility in study as the great advantage of internet-based education. But the cost of student flexibility is staff productivity. The major justification for staff to promote internet-based education is that it "increase[s] students' responsibility of their own learning." The point of assessment is to regulate the learning of students who cannot regulate their own progress. However student evaluations demonstrate that the reverse is actually taking place.

The desire for flexibility, as a justification for the increasing role of the internet in teaching, is at the loss of other, older imperatives of university education. Similarly, the aspiration for excellence is part of managerial vocationalism, and a denial of both the cultural imperative of citizenship and the social justice focus of the post-war university.

The point of flexibility was — politically — highly useful. It was a way to transform universities into sites of lifelong learning. It has now transformed into a strategy to retract three-year degrees, take course overloads and cheapen what is being taught.

Learning always exists in a social situation. The application of that knowledge creates a link between doing and thinking. This connectiveness can occur in any media at any time. However, it does take intellectual discipline on the behalf of the student. Learning — challenging learning — is rarely pleasant. It is confronting to re-theorise the truths impressed from parents, friends, religious organisations and governments.

The stakeholders in technology education are myriad: from governments to university administrators and employers. Yet it is the teachers who must make the virtual classroom—with all its practicalities — actually function. The aim of corporate capitalism is to "minimise the uncertainties of the free market by attempting to regularise relations with customers." Information architecture must be developed with clear purposes, necessitating precise decisions about content. Institutional decisions must be made about standard metadata and cost-effective system expansion. These are "top-down" decisions: hardly promoting the egalitarianism of the internet.

Literacy and Cultural Capital

Literacy standards have been a tenet of neo-liberal ideologies. It is the force that invades and transforms an oral culture. Therefore, the changes of literacy invoke compromises to both the humanities and the educational system. It is difficult to reconcile the fetishisation of literacy with the contemporary reality of how information is created, stored, applied and distributed.

The corporate aims of the university signal a movement from cultural capital to dollars and cents. Western institutionalised education has built civilisation by advancing industrialisation. In times of rapid social change, workforce skills lag behind best practice. University teachers have to link students' abilities, hopes and desires with the conformity of the workplace. It is assumed that students know how to read before they enter a library. The process for attaining these skills is still in development.

Issues of Teacher Bandwidth

When bandwidth issues are discussed in the context of online learning, one frequently thinks of the speed with which a large amount of data can make its way to students' homes. In the past five years broadband deployment has increased significantly, and it is possible that eventually there may be high speed internet access generally available in student homes. The idea of "teacher bandwidth" analogises students to data, and teachers to pipes, and formulates the problem thus: how many students can a teacher support in an online learning environment?

While some distance education organisations see the internet as an opportunity to expand their student base to hundreds of thousands of students, providing feedback and learning support for such large numbers is problematic. In contrast to classroom learning, these approaches enable the pace, sequence, content and method of instruction to better fit each student's learning style, objectives and goals. The dilemma presented by individually tailored instruction is that it combines an instructional imperative with an economic impossibility.

Instructional technology promises to provide most of the advantages of individualised instruction at affordable cost while maintaining consistent, measurable, high-quality content. Following are the approaches to solving the scalability or "teacher bandwidth" problem:

i) A one-on-one instructional model in which a teacher tailors instruction to individual student needs is preferable to other instructional models,

ii) Human (teacher-student) interaction in large scale learning environments is not economically feasible, therefore

iii) Automating feedback and other learning support via intelligent instructional systems is the only viable solution to providing scalable online learning. How does an organisation scale to provide individualised learning support to large numbers of students? The solution that is becoming increasingly popular replaces human teachers with intelligent, automated systems. These systems sequence instructional modules or "learning objects" for users in real time according to intelligent algorithms, and provide predefined or "intelligent" feedback based on assessments of learners.

While a significant amount of energy and financing has gone into the automated learning objects approach to overcoming the teacher bandwidth problem, it suffers from a number of critical weaknesses.

i) Automated instructional systems completely lack human interaction and social negotiation, which learning theorists are increasingly stressing as crucial to supporting meaningful learning .

ii) Highly decontextualised learning objects are reusable in the greatest number of learning contexts, but they are also the most expensive and difficult for instructional designers to reuse, creating a "reusability paradox"

iii) Computers are currently incapable of participating in the very human meaning-making activities required of instructional design and development based on fine-grained components.

Online Self-Organising Social Systems (OSOSS)

Online self-organising social systems (OSOSS) are facilitated by a particular type of software infrastructure, one that is generally web-based and characterised by a high degree of management decentralisation. The website genre known as the "web log" or "blog" is such an infrastructure, and provides a fertile primordial soup from which online self-organising social systems can emerge.

The day-to-day tasks of creating new content, adding commentary, evaluating the quality of submitted material, providing user support and answering questions, and other tasks are distributed across the entire community via the blog infrastructure. OSOSS vary in the degree of decentralisation they employ, the content domain they cover, and the explicitness of their learning facilitation. While none of the existing OSOSS consider themselves learning communities, learning is happening among their users, and happening in an extremely innovative manner.

The moderation system evolved in order to help the community self-sustain. Meta-moderation evolved in response to similar needs. One can easily imagine a number of circumstances that would have prevented this adaptation, resulting in the death of the system. In their ability to self-maintain while preserving their identity, OSOSS are autopoietic. Since learning objects mediate the activities of individuals within an OSOSS, it stands to reason that the structure may be susceptible to the same weaknesses as the traditional methods of using learning objects.

The most significant departure of the OSOSS from conventional learning objects approaches is that it relies on human beings to locate, assemble, and contextualise the resources. When learning objects are considered as mediational means that learners employ in problem solving and other types of activity, seemingly heterogeneous digital content chunks, assessments, simulations, and applications rotate into a single mediational factor. OSOSS provide a conceptual framework for a new method of indexing, discovering, combining, using, and evaluating digital educational resources.

Indexing and discovery: Learning objects are not catalogued with metadata and submitted to a central curator repository. Community members know of existing resources and local resource collections. Individual resources are discovered through "community queries" in which community members respond with pointers to resources they know about personally.

Combination: Learning objects are not automatically populated into one of many instructional templates. Without the direction of any single grand architect, peers contribute relevant resources and descriptions of how they might be employed within the context of the initiator's problem. Much like a colony of ants, peers autonomously build on one another's work and create a satisficing resource structure without centralised direction .

Use: Learners do not sit through a temporal sequencing of resources and assessments linked to decontextualised instructional objectives. They employ resources provided by peers as mediational means in the solution of a self-selected problem or accomplishment of another self-selected goal.

Evaluation: Learners evaluate the relevance and suitability of resources within a specific learning context.

Like any other instructional technology, the success of OSOSS in facilitating learning will depend on the degree to which instructional design principles are obeyed, whether this obedience is conscious or otherwise on the part of the learner. OSOSS are no more the "cure to all instructional ills" than any predecessor instructional technology has been. And while they have the potential to improve online learning in meaningful ways, OSOSS lacks a number of characteristics that are considered "strengths" of automated instructional approaches. Following are the future challenges of OSOSS:

i) A standard curriculum may be difficult to impose on individuals in an OSOSS.

ii) Assessment of individuals may be difficult to carry out in an OSOSS.

iii) Required feedback may not be immediate in an OSOSS.

Assessment of Online learning

Assessment is an integral part of learning. It needs to be planned at the stage when the learning strategies are being developed. Assessing online involves the same rules as all other forms of assessment: it needs to be valid, reliable, flexible and fair. However, being in its relative infancy, some concerns have been evinced; for example, the increased possibilities for cheating. But this can be overcome by designing assessment processes appropriately. Online approaches seem to be used more extensively for formative than summative assessment.

In formative assessment, which helps learners monitor their learning, quizzes, true/false questions and item banks are being used extensively to check learning progress. In summative assessment, where judgements about competence are made, email is being used for the submission of assignments and providing feedback, but it is generally acknowledged that there is a way to go before this form of assessment is used effectively and to its full potential online.

Learner-centred assessment approaches, which include peer, group and self-assessment, create further opportunities for assessment processes online while assisting in the development of collaborative skills and other essential workplace and life skills. The objective is to make assessment a much more integrated and transparent process which can be supported by the new technologies, creating portfolios of evidence, developing assessment criteria available to all, and generating opportunities for a greater role to be taken by the learners themselves.

Nevertheless, a range of forms of evidence is needed to assess competence accurately, and online will not be appropriate for them all. Therefore a blend of off- and online assessment approaches may be utilised, the choice of approach being influenced by learner needs and access to technology, available resources, the nature of the discipline area being assessed and most importantly what is to be assessed.

Following are the list of pedagogical effectiveness indicators for online delivery of vocational education and training.

Learning-related effectiveness are:

i) a learner-centred environment
ii) teaching and learning strategies which develop cognitive skills
iii) high levels of interactivity between all participants
iv) engagement with the online materials
v) learning experiences which encourage synthesis and analysis
vi) opportunities for 'deep learning'

Teaching related effectiveness are:

i) approaches enabling learners to build new knowledge and skills based on what they already have (constructivist approaches)
ii) consistent levels of feedback
iii) thoughtful matches between materials, learning styles and learning contexts
iv) a model of delivery that includes thorough planning, monitoring, reviewing and evaluating course materials and student progress
v) teachers who are imaginative, flexible, technologically gymnastic, committed, responsible and expert communicators.

Materials and resource related effectiveness are:

i) high-quality materials design
ii) a range of available navigational choices for students.

Technology related effectiveness are:

i) guaranteed and reliable forms of access to the technology

ii) quick and easy access to the training site and the online technology

It is suggested that these are ideals but that practice rarely conforms fully to these principles. The dominating influence of the technology has created assumptions about the nature of learning, the role of the teacher and the student characteristics that do not match well with teacher and learner expectations and/or experiences. Communication, interactivity and the development of strong links between those who are learning and teaching are very important.

Effective teacher-student relationships are regarded as a critical success factor to develop in an online environment. The effective student learning online requires teaching and learning environments where students have the opportunity to:

i) reduce their reliance on text

ii) explore and value their intellectual, social and cultural backgrounds

iii) develop their knowledge beyond the transmission and assessment of content

iv) reflect on their own learning

v) be part of an inclusive learning environment

vi) communicate extensively with their peers and their teachers

vii) become self-regulated and engaged with their own learning

viii) develop a group identity that connects them with their learning and with the broader social environment.

Barriers of Effective Online Learning

The greatest deterrents to a high-quality online learning experience for students are problems with technology and access to the internet. For students, barriers can include bandwidth, fast and affordable internet access, speed of software and access to uptodate equipment. Significant issues which may also constitute barriers include the level of technical support available, their literacy and IT skills and other aptitudes.

Equity of access needs to be kept in mind as these technologies and learning approaches can exclude many who are on low incomes or who may not be in work. Others live where the maintenance of a reliable and high-speed connection to the internet is problematic, such as rural and remote areas. In a world becoming increasingly dependent on computer technologies and access to information and knowledge there is a danger that, while online learning will open doors for some, others will become further marginalised.

For teachers, barriers relate to their ability to use the technology in ways which support a student-centred and facilitation approach to teaching and the institutional structures in which they work. The fact is that many structures and policies are still based on an assumption of face-to-face delivery.

Online learning is sometimes defined more narrowly but it is most properly seen as a way of contributing to solving learning problems faced by individuals and enterprises in the most expeditious way, by enhancing, extending or replacing traditional teaching and training practices. It offers and enhances flexibility and options so that the learning is potentially of the highest quality. But it also needs to be more 'whole of organisation' so that it provides access to appropriate and comprehensive student support systems, information and other services.

Online delivery needs to be set within appropriate pedagogical and business frameworks. Greater use could be made of induction programmes (awareness of technology, how to use technology interactively, the conventions associated with technology usage) to ensure that all students who enrol in courses are prepared for the use of online approaches. Induction programmes should also cover study skills. Programmes such as these may help to reduce unnecessary attrition and assist students to develop the 'technical' and other 'soft' skills they need to enable them to focus on learning, rather than focusing on mastering the technology.

Costs can be reduced by such strategies as redesigning work processes to change how student support is delivered; for example: using different people to deal with relatively simple helpdesk queries integrating back office systems for managing student enrolments, payment processes and other services, as well as tracking student progress having instructors use automated response systems to reduce time spent on dealing with individual queries or making use of synchronous discussion groups to make it easier for students to help each other.

Online learning is just one component of an integrated e-business approach, whereby organisations can use the opportunities provided by these technologies to improve systems, reduce costs where appropriate, and work in more integrated and effective ways. Traditionally, administrative and support processes have been kept largely separate from those concerned with teaching and learning.

There are significant risks associated with e-business and privacy invasions and legal issues also need to be addressed when embedding online learning within an e-business approach. It is therefore no simple matter to merge online learning and e-business. The secret to success lies in good planning. Adopting an e-business solution which meets the provider's—but especially its customers'—needs offers a way of achieving these business goals. But to do this, and to make the teaching and learning experience better, some things about the ways both staff and providers work need to change.

Models of Online Learning

Today, there are new ways of using information technology to enhance the process of teaching and learning and to extend access to new populations of students. For most institutions, however, new technologies represent a black hole of additional expense. Most campuses have simply bolted new technologies onto a fixed plant, a fixed faculty, and a fixed notion of classroom instruction. Under these circumstances, technology becomes part of the problem of rising costs rather than part of the solution.

All of the redesign projects make the teaching-learning enterprise significantly more active and learner-centred. Lectures are replaced with a variety of learning resources that move students from a passive, note-taking role to an active, learning orientation. Instructional software and other web-based learning resources assume an important role in engaging students with course content. Resources include tutorials, exercises, and low-stakes quizzes that provide frequent practice, feedback, and reinforcement of course concepts.

The redesign projects add greater flexibility for when students can engage with a course, but the redesigned courses are not self-paced. Rather than depending on class meetings, student pacing and progress are organised by the need to master specific learning objectives, which are frequently in modular format, according to scheduled milestones for completion. An expanded support system enables students to receive assistance from a variety of different people.

By constructing support systems consisting of various kinds of instructional personnel, the projects apply the right level of human intervention to particular student problems. All projects have these characteristics in common, each has chosen a design model that implements the characteristics in a way that varies according to the discipline involved, the particular student audience, and the preferences of faculty. These common characteristics are arrayed in the various projects, there are five distinct course-redesign models: supplemental, replacement, emporium, fully online, and buffet.

The supplemental model

The supplemental model retains the basic structure of the traditional course, particularly the number of class meetings. Some of the supplemental redesigns simply add technology-based, out-of-class activities to encourage greater student engagement with course content. Others change what goes on in the class meetings as well as adding out-of-class activities.

Students are encouraged to take the quizzes as many times as needed until they attain a perfect score. For all quizzes, only the highest scores count. The more time students spend taking quizzes and the higher their scores, the better they perform on in-class exams. A two-disc CD-ROM, which contains interactive activities, simulations, and movies, is used to review and augment text material.

The goal is to create an active learning environment within a large lecture hall setting supplemented by a variety of out-of-class activities that ensure students are prepared when they come to class. To assess their preparation for class, students then complete online quizzes, which provide immediate feedback to students and data for instructors to assess students' knowledge levels. Instructors are able to reduce class time spent on topics that the students clearly understand, increase time spent on problem areas, and target individual students for remedial help.

Class time is divided into ten- to fifteen-minute lecture segments followed by sessions in which students work in small groups applying concepts to solve problems posed by the instructor. The instructor moderates the discussions and draws out key issues to reinforce specific ideas or reveal misconceptions. Redesigning in-class activities has encouraged students to come to class; in turn, this increased attendance has had a positive effect on student learning.

Before the meeting, the instructor uses software to review all the posted written answers to a given question. Periodically, the instructor poses a related question and gives the class time for each team to formulate an answer.

The replacement model

The key characteristic of the replacement model is a reduction in class-meeting time, replacing face-to-face time with online, interactive learning activities for students. The assumption is that certain activities can be better accomplished online, either individually or in small groups, than in a class. In some cases, out-of-class activities take place in computer labs; in others, they occur online so that students can participate anytime, anywhere.

One version of the replacement model replaces some class meetings with online activities while keeping in-class activities more or less the same. Others replace some class meetings with online activities and also make significant changes in what goes on in the remaining class meetings. Rather than assuming that face-to-face meetings are the best setting for student learning, these projects have thought about why classes need to meet in real time and the content of that meeting in relation to the desired learning outcomes.

In the computer-studio labs, students work individually and collaboratively on prepared activities. Approximately 30 per cent of the lab time is used for elaboration of concepts, 60 per cent for computer-related work and class discussion of the results, and 10 percent for online quizzes on concepts related to the activities. Students are regularly tested on assigned readings and homework using Readiness Assessment Tests (RATs), short quizzes that probe students' conceptual understanding.

RATs are given five to seven times during the course. Students prepare to take the RATs outside of class by reading the textbook, completing homework assignments, and using web-based resources. Students then take the tests individually. Immediately following the individual effort, the students take the same test in groups of four. In addition to motivating students to keep on top of the course material, RATs have proven to be very effective in detecting areas in which students are not grasping the concepts, enabling faculty to take corrective actions in a timely manner.

Students particularly like the ability to link directly from a problem they have difficulty with to a tutorial that helps them learn the concepts needed to solve the problem.

Students receive immediate feedback and detailed explanations in response to their online work, and class time is freed for interactive and collaborative learning experiences. Online grading has given the instructors more time to prepare their classes and to focus on meaningful communicative and collaborative tasks in class. By making these changes, both universities have been able to increase the time that students spend in oral communication. Furthermore, they have been able to increase the number of students who can be served with the same personnel resources.

The emporium model

The redesign model allows students to choose when to access course materials, what types of learning materials to use depending on their needs, and how quickly to work through the materials with the support of sophisticated instructional software and one-on-one on-site help. The emporium model eliminates all class meetings and replaces them with a learning resource centre featuring online materials and on-demand personalised assistance. The model requires a significant commitment of space and equipment.

The emporium model is heavily dependent on instructional software, including interactive tutorials, computational exercises, electronic hyper-textbooks, practice exercises, solutions to frequently asked questions, and online quizzes. Modularised online tutorials present course content with links to a variety of additional learning tools: streaming-video lectures, lecture notes, and exercises. Navigation is interactive; students can choose to see additional explanation and examples along the way. Online weekly practice quizzes replace weekly homework grading. With the development of a server-based testing system, large databases of questions are easily generated, and grading and record-keeping are automatic.

The fully online model

On most campuses, the job of a faculty member is seen as monolithic: to perform a collection of tasks that are, with few exceptions, carried out alone. In most colleges and universities, this repetitive, labour-intensive approach has been transferred to online education as well. Individual faculty members design and deliver multiple course sections, each of which is relatively small in size. Web-based materials are used largely as supplemental resources rather than as substitutes for direct instruction.

The buffet model

Students need to be treated like individuals, rather than homogenous groups, and should be offered many more learning options within each course. Rather than maintaining a fixed view of what all students want or what all students need, institutions need to be flexible and create environments that enable greater choice for students. Students differ in the amount of interaction that they require with faculty, staff, and one another.

Since students learn in different ways, even the best "fixed menu" of teaching strategies will fail for some students. Students receive an initial in-class orientation that provides information about the buffet structure, the course content, the learning contract, the purpose of the learning styles and study skills assessments, and the various ways that they might choose to learn the material. Out of class, they complete online learning styles and study skills instruments and receive a report of their results, as well as directions on how to use this information to build the online course contract. Students are initially given a set of default, software-generated study options to match their learning styles and study skills; these options can be changed according to students' preferences.

Although these models have demonstrated that they can successfully improve the quality of student learning while reducing the cost of instruction, each of these models tends to be attached to one way of doing things and treats all students as if they were the same. In essence, like the traditional classroom model, these course-redesign models represent a one-size-fits-all approach, albeit a much improved one.

Yet one of the strongest reasons for using information technology in teaching and learning is that it can radically increase the array of learning possibilities presented to each individual student. Thus, the "right way" to design a high-quality course depends entirely on the type of students involved. By customising the learning environment for each student, institutions are likely to achieve greater learning successes.

Learning Outcomes

The changing nature of the world's economic system—the shift from an industry-based society to an information-based society—is a pervasive factor driving educational changes for people of all ages. Society is shifting to the application of knowledge as the primary means of raising productivity. In an information-based society, knowledge work is the primary mode of work, since information provides the primary means by which work is accomplished. This presents qualitatively different challenges to traditional companies. Innovative companies are responding to these challenges by transforming into learning organisations.

Effective knowledge workers need to develop new higher-level skills for accessing, selecting, manipulating, and representing information in a variety of formats. But this alone is not sufficient. As George Leonard said in 1968, "The highly technological, regenerative society now emerging will require something akin to mass genius, mass creativity, and lifelong learning." That vision of a quarter-century ago is now reality. We are facing the challenge of large-scale knowledge production. Schools, in turn, can respond to this challenge by taking seriously the constructivist approach to learning. If children and teachers are engaged, collaboratively, in actively constructing their own knowledge, then schools are laying a foundation for the intellectual development of the knowledge worker.

Examples of students and teachers contributing to the information infrastructure by producing authentic products that represent their growing skills and knowledge are explored in this section.

Collaborative Inquiry

Collaborative inquiry in networked communities is a genre of learning, teaching, and knowledge-creating activity that illustrates many elements of educational reform and the knowledge-based society. Students in schools gather data from their local environments, such as acidity of their rain water, quality of the indoor air, ozone levels, water quality in rivers and streams, biological indicators of changes in climate or pollution, effects of ultraviolet light on plant and animal life, species diversity, wildlife populations, and migration patterns. They work in teams, often engaging parents and other local community members in their investigations. Each team is also part of a virtual community of scientists, students, and teachers in other schools.

Each school contributes to a collective database that includes information from many different geographic locations. Through the networks, the students work together to aggregate, analyse, and interpret the data and share their discoveries and interpretations. The large database gives students the opportunity to recognise geographic patterns in the data and provides a basis for comparing local data with data from other locations; data gathered locally now have more value because it is shared with a geographically distributed community.

There are hundreds of such collaborative inquiry projects and communities organised by teachers, experts, and students. Such projects help students move between the concrete, physical world they can touch and measure, and the electronic world of data they analyse to make and communicate powerful abstractions. By learning to observe and describe their local physical and social world in ways useful to people in other locations, they learn to create knowledge, a role that in earlier times was enjoyed by only the small minority of scientists, inventors, writers, industrialists, or statesmen. In these kinds of collaborative inquiry communities, the learner has a real and responsive audience. This is highly motivating, just as it is motivating to any professional to get feedback from colleagues or audiences.

Global Lab project

Over the past several years, teachers and researchers have begun developing tools and standard methods that help make virtual communities more productive. In the Global Lab project organised by TERC, teachers, high school students, and research scientists around the world study local and global ecological change. They use low-cost instruments and sensors such as ozonometers, ion-selective probes for soil and water monitoring, and field data loggers.

To make meaningful scientific comparisons with sites from around the world, students and teachers must ensure that all factors influencing measurements are identical; when students in Moscow and Boston establish uniform guidelines to compare data, they learn the rigours and excitement of research. Students learn to investigate trends, compare their findings with local regulations and standards, and report and analyse data. The use of common instruments and software helps establish a common basis for collaboration. A peer review system, access to scientists for online assistance, and participation in collaborative research groups help develop quality research projects. Much work needs to be done in establishing mechanisms for maintaining quality of the knowledge produced.

Project GLOBE

Since they are located all over the world, schoolchildren can often monitor many more sites for environmental studies than the professional scientific community could support. This is the basic idea of the GLOBE project initiated by Gore, the then Vice President of USA. Eventually, when large numbers of students and teachers have the appropriate tools, skills, and network participation, they will fill an important role in areas such as monitoring atmospheric ozone, ultraviolet light, water pollution, soil pollution, and bioindicators of global, regional, and local change. The economic value of students' work has already been recognised by some of the companies that produce instruments and sensors. These companies value data collected in diverse circumstances and locations for testing their products; the companies provide the products to the community at reduced prices.

Systems Thinking

At Gonzaga High School in Washington D.C., students and their teachers are creating an internet world wide web server on the subject of earth system science. Students use systems modeling software (STELLA II), data visualisation tools (NCSA Image and NCSA Collage), and data from NASA databases to research earth system science topics. In each project, the students conduct background research, create hypotheses, develop a strategy for data search, investigation, and testing, model the system qualitatively and quantitatively, and communicate their findings through a hypermedia document using NCSA Mosaic on the internet. The teachers are collaborating with teachers in other D.C. schools to form an exchange of such models and course materials through their internet server.

Foundation for a Participatory Vision of Education

The following characteristics of active learning provide a foundation for a participatory vision of education:

i) bringing learning into a closer relationship to the real-world context of problems and projects;
ii) working collaboratively with peers and mentors;
iii) engendering closer relationships between people inside schools and outside in the "real world";
iv) working in a hands-on mode with the physical world, in addition to working with symbols and words;
v) learning something just at the time it is needed to solve a problem or complete a project, rather than in a preset curriculum sequence;
vi) learning in an interdisciplinary context, rather than always separating subjects into isolated topics;
vii) working on a problem in depth, rather than covering many topics superficially;
viii) for teachers, becoming guides and mentors and learners, too, rather than only dispensers of knowledge;
ix) constructing one's own knowledge rather than memorising facts from authorities;

x) working on projects and problems of intrinsic interest to the learner or a group of learners, rather than learning what everyone else of the same age is expected to learn at the time;

xi) building learning experiences on the learning one does throughout life,

xii) rather than only on "school" subjects;

xiii) basing assessment on performance of real tasks rather than on artificial tests;

xiv) using the real tools for intellectual work that are used in the workplace, rather than oversimplified textbook techniques; and

xv) working directly with people from other places and cultures, rather than only learning about other places indirectly through books.

Creating this kind of foundation will be a collaborative effort or partnership among administrators, university faculty members, community, business, labour, and political leaders, as well as parents, teachers, and students.

The central value of internetworking to support learning and teaching for our changing world is that internetworking can support or enable authentic learning experiences and cross-institutional collaborations needed for the reform of education.

The people who use the internet are creating and exchanging knowledge, rather than passively receiving someone else's information. There is a danger that the networks could be used to transmit and amplify traditional and outmoded elements of schooling instead of providing a mechanism for the transformation to lifelong learning needed by all citizens.

How we shape and engineer the technology, tools, organisation of knowledge, and virtual communities on the expanding internet information infrastructure will directly affect the potential productivity, roles, and equity of opportunity of young people in the near and distant future, and thereby will affect the kind of society into which we evolve.

Learner and teacher contributions to the current internet provide a glimpse of what is possible with today's technology, infrastructure, and organisational arrangements. However, the value that people can contribute and the value that they get is limited by the local networking infrastructure, tools, and services on the internet, and by the free-for-all nature of the interactions on most current virtual communities. Most contributions wind up as flotsam and jetsam on a vast chaotic sea of e-mail, newsgroup messages, and web pages—with little order, discipline, quality assessment, structure, retrievability, review, or aggregation.

There has been considerable recent progress in developing software that makes it easier to get onto the networks and discover information from personal computers. As more people attempt to participate and more virtual communities are formed, we are gaining more insight into the kinds of tools and services needed for full participation, including user construction of knowledge and information services.

Many factors affect the value of contributions made by individuals and groups. In the US National School Network Testbed, BBN is collaborating with over 100 organisations that are exploring models for leveraging internet access for educational innovation.

Scaling up is not a simple matter of physically connecting more people and organisations to the internet. Rather, scaling up has many dimensions—technical, organisational, educational, economic, and social. If internet working supports the transformation outlined here, then "scaling up" has to mean all these things, and more. Decisions made by government agencies, corporations, and communities about investment in infrastructure and educational reform will take into account the mechanisms needed to make progress on all of these fronts.

The following four-part vision may help to guide our decision-making, particularly with regard to elementary and secondary education in the future:

i) *Responsibility for one's learning will be shared by all:* The pace of change is too fast for individuals to depend totally on others to structure their learning and information for them; pre-planned courses, textbooks, teacher training programmes, technical support staff, and the like may not always be available to meet an individual's particular learning need. New curriculum frameworks, instructional materials, assessment and testing schemes, and teacher training programmes will take into account these increased responsibilities for information management and knowledge creation. Similarly, software and networked information services for educational purposes will be designed with the assumption that people will be taking on these responsibilities.

   In the quest for ease of use of information and tools in the internet, we must be careful not to exclude people from participating in the more complex and rewarding tasks of constructing knowledge. Students will learn how to deal with phenomena that are new and more complex than they are "ready" for, and will have opportunities to make sense out of situations before they understand all the first principles.

ii) *Responsibility for teaching and mentoring will be shared more widely than in the past*: Classroom teachers will not be expected to have expertise in all the areas of knowledge their students are encountering. The communications networks will support teaching by people whose primary work is not formally teaching, but who have expertise in industry and other public sectors. Incentives to perform these part-time and out-of- school teaching and mentoring roles will be devised. Communities and school districts making an investment in new curricula or technology should not attempt to overlay such innovations on outmoded methods of operation of schools; rather, they will look broadly for new opportunities to engage people in nontraditional roles.

iii) *Learning is seen more as a process*: Intelligence is recognised as diversified, and authentic assessment tells us to look at it in context. Teachers and administrators are also learners. In that role they are typical learning organisation managers. They are mentors; they guide, provide access to resources, facilitate. School itself is a more integrated system. School is divided into smaller clusters, where teachers and students and their families get to know one another and form a sense of community. Collaborative groups work on meaningful projects, and just-in-time seminars and workshops provide support for the projects.

i) *Educational reforms will evolve in synchrony with the evolving information infrastructure:* As a society, we are working hard on educational reform at the same time that we are evolving a new information infrastructure. There is a danger that the enormous efforts now put into educational "reforms" will turn out to be irrelevant to the circumstances of learning and working in a networked, knowledge-creating society. Current investments in reformed curriculum frameworks, standards, assessments, teacher in-service programmes, and the like should take advantage of networking to reduce industrial-age constraints.

References

Anderson, L.M. and Ching, M., *Affective Teacher Education: International Encyclopaedia of Teaching and Teacher Education*, Pergamon Press, New York, 1987.

Goyal B.R., *Multigrade Teaching: In-service Education Package for Elementary Teacher Educators,* NCERT, New Delhi, 1992.

______________ , 1992, *Multigrade Teaching: In-service Education Package for Elementary Teacher Educators,* NCERT, New Delhi.

Kaufman, D., "Constructivist-based experiential learning in teacher education", *Action in Teacher Education* 18(2), 40-49, EJ 536 845, 1996.

Patil, V.T, Dubey, S. N., *Inservice Education for Teachers,* Authorspress, New Delhi, 2001

Richardson, V., "Constructivist teaching and teacher education: Theory and practice", In V. Richardson (ed.), *Constructivist Teacher Education: Building New Understandings*, Washington, DC: Falmer Press, 1997.

9

Transformation of Learning in Networked World

During the last half-century, information technology has infiltrated our lives at an unprecedented rate. In education, it took the form of "audiovisual aids". Ever since, much has been said about the potential for technology to "revolutionise" teaching and learning. Instructional technology, whether "hard" or "soft", does not operate in isolation. It is used by teachers and students; it is affected by infrastructure issues like classroom design and network connectivity; it is bought by support staff at the direction of administrators with funding from school boards who are elected by parents. These information technologies are part of an educational system, and are interdependent with all other parts.

When technology is introduced "in isolation", it disturbs the rest of the system. The resulting instability reduces the system's overall effectiveness. In an effort to restore the system to its previous state, its other components exert pressure on the changed subsystem to conform to their requirements. Consequently, the change is usually not implemented as its proponents envisioned.

Current educational systems are optimised for an industrial society, where selection, rather than learning, was the overriding objective. Society required owners, managers, labourers, and schools had to "presort" the future workforce into these categories. Today, however, we live in an information based society. Increasingly, even blue-collar jobs require acquisition and analysis of complex information, rather than rote task performance. In fact, this entire task-based paradigm is an Industrial Age construct of limited utility in today's environment.

In the Information Age, there are not nearly as many activities where rote performance of a known set of steps in a fixed order is effective. Instead, today's world demands critical thinking and on-the-fly problem solving. Today, world wide web (WWW) as a research tool in the curriculum. Technology has a facilitating or enabling role in each of these suggested changes, but if it is to be successful and enduring, its introduction must be synchronised with the organisational, procedural, and philosophical changes these changes imply.

Interactive Learning Within Computer Networks

Interactive learning can be defined as "learner-centred learning using a multimedia approach." In this process one finds several kinds of interaction between:

i) teachers and learners
ii) conventional media (print-based materials)
iii) computer-based media (hypertext, hypermedia, optical discs, networks, etc.).

In true interaction it is understood that a student, to a certain degree, changes the learning process which interchanges the roles of a student and a teacher.

Interactive learning was born from CBT and interactive video, in an effort to compensate for the existing drawbacks. Programmed instruction, CAI, CAL, CBT, and interactive video represent an extension of the linear book metaphor, and thus computers have not been able to completely replace the role of a book, which is still a dominant medium in education. This may account for poor success of these educational methods, likewise, the effort to use a computer as a "teaching machine" that would teach students more efficiently and faster than a teacher. Today, developments in computer use in education are focused in the direction of a "learning machine" and interactive multimedia.

It was as early as 1945 that Vannevar Bush has, in his essay "As We May Think" in the July issue of *The Atlantic Monthly* predicted the use of interactive multimedia as he pioneered the concept of hypertext (of course, at the time he lacked the technology to implement it). Bush describes a machine called "Memex" (Memory Extender) which allows user to store data and create, and later use, hypertext links between data by the principle of associative indexing.

The word "hypertext" was, however, introduced by Ted Nelson in the 60's. He has envisioned a society in which online hypertext documents are as common as books or magazines are today. Very soon, the notion of linking content was applied to graphics, sound, animation and video which gave birth to the concept of hypermedia. However, it was only recently that this idea could be materialised, when adequate technology became available.

Hypertext and hypermedia systems enable teachers to create learning materials through which students can navigate according to their own abilities and interests. In addition, at the highest level of interaction, the students can create their own materials and link it with these created by the teacher. •

The idea of education based on learning and not teaching has intrigued cognitive psychologists and educators. They have studied the ways in which people learn in order to find best forms of presenting knowledge which could be used in developing materials for individual interactive learning. It has been shown that it is easier to learn and remember material presented in graphical form, and when learning it requires more activity on students' part.

Another way of learning is learning through the use of goal-based scenarios — the teacher sets the learning goals and each student researches the subject in his or her own way, discussing it later with colleagues. In this way students are more mentally involved which results in better understanding and learning of the material.

Studies have shown that the use of hypermedia, not only improves student's motivation for learning, but also improves the student's ability to make his own cognitive connections, handle large amounts of information, use critical, relational thinking, participate in class discussions, and ability to read.

What makes the use of interactive multimedia courseware in education particularly attractive is "individualisation of instruction, self-paced exploration of knowledge, experimental learning, and instant and effortless performance measurement." This helps develop new ways of thinking and drawing conclusions in students who use interactive multimedia for experiments and simulations, making them "symbolic analysts" capable of interpreting reality in abstract terms and then manipulating them using analytic tools.

How much the advantages of interactive multimedia will be visible depends on how the courseware is adopted to students that use it. It has been expected that the use of interactive multimedia in schools will grow because of its above discussed advantages, as well as because of drop in cost of hardware and multimedia software making it more affordable.

In the beginning of the 1990's it was predicted that the digital compact disc (CD), which had replaced analogue interactive video, would become the main publishing medium for interactive learning, and that it would be used throughout the world. Today, beside courseware in traditional "stand-alone" form on CD, the distribution is more and more common over computer networks. A particular role in this process has the web. Website can look like a page of some multimedia document on a CD-ROM, but it additionally offers a connection with computers throughout the world, thus creating a new dimension of cyberspace. This makes interactive learning and teaching using multimedia/hypermedia within computer networks of special interest in contemporary education.

Networking, and closely related mobility, together with multimedia represent main technologies which, if correctly used, can advance education. Networking includes LANs, WANs, online services and especially internet, together with all supported applications such as e-mail, navigation services, audio- and video-conferencing, and collaborative software. Mobility is a form of networking where connectivity is achieved through "wireless LANs", and thus students can borrow notebook computers from their schools, and using them can access courseware or communicate with their teachers or among themselves. The combination of networking and mobile access has particularly contributed to the development of distance learning.

Use of distance learning and learning on demand started in the 1970's, to allow students that attended the university while working, follow courses without coming on campus. Distance learning systems are based on digital video technology. They allow capturing lectures in real time, storing the compressed video on a central on-demand server, and transmitting the compressed video in real time over local and wide area networks to local servers or to individual desktop computers in libraries, laboratories, and remote customer sites.

Whatever technology is used in distance education, a virtual classroom is always the aspiration. In this virtual classroom students need not gather at the same physical place at the same time, while the same, or even better, learning effects may be obtained. Today more common are WWW-based distance education system that aims to provide an integrated and distributed hypermedia information environment for the academic community. In this environment, instructors can construct course material and prepare some learning assistance for learners; learners can access course material and participate in online and off-line discussion using WWW browsers.

Recently, videoconferencing has also been used in distance education. Due to the limitations of the performance of the host computer and the network bandwidth, desktop videoconferencing is still an emerging technology, which is more used in a closed environment, but it is expected that it will be used in the future to connect companies, educational institutions and homes.

Educational Applications of Internet

One of the most complete overviews of the use of internet in education was given by Harris. She differentiates between three kinds of so called telecollaborative educational activities, each of which is divided in several activities:

i) *Interpersonal exchanges*—individuals talk electronically to other individuals, individuals talk to groups, or groups talk to other groups:

  a) *Keypals*—students communicate among themselves, and normally choose the topic of discussion, which enables them to learn about other cultures through direct contact with other students.

  b) *Global classrooms*—communication between two or more classes about the common topic; more directed to given topic than Keypals and engages groups of students rather than individuals.

  c) *Electronic appearances*—a guest communicates with students via e-mail, newsgroups, or BBS asynchronously, or in real-time (electronic events).

  d) *Electronic mentoring*—experts from universities, industry, government, etc., help students to research particular topics.

  e) *Question-and-answer services*

  f) *Impersonations* — users that participate in such projects play a role of another person, such as historic personalities or characters from literature.

ii) *Information collections* — collecting, compiling and comparing information:

  a) *Information exchanges* — students and teachers from the entire world collect and send information (cultural exchange).

b) *Database creation* — collection and organisation of data in DB's which can be shared with other internet users via, say, the WWW.

c) *Electronic publishing* — production of magazines.

d) *Telefieldtrips* — students and teachers share observations and experiences from field trips; experts can report on expeditions.

e) *Pooled data analyses* — collected data are analysed, statistically processed, and presented.

iii) *Problem-solving projects* — one of the most beneficial educational opportunities that we can offer to students:

a) *Information searches* — students are given a riddle/ problem and solve it using the given references (in electronic or printed format).

b) *Electronic process writing* — writing poetry, essays, etc., which are published on the net.

c) *Sequential creations* — collaborative creation of text and pictures, synchronously or asynchronously, by students from different locations using the internet.

d) *Parallel problem solving* — similar problem is given to students in different locations; the students solve the problems individually and later exchange the solutions and methods electronically.

e) *Virtual gatherings* — gathers participants from different geographical locations and time zones in real-time in a form of "computer mediated meeting".

f) *Simulations* — students participate in online simulations.

e) *Social action projects* — participation in humanitarian, ecological, and similar projects.

Educational Applications of World Wide Web

The web was primarily developed out of a need to share technical and corporate information at colleges, universities and research institutions, but it was quickly shown that it could be used in education, especially for open and distance learning. The WWW can be viewed as a source of edutainment that is effective in the entertainment side because most students are highly motivated to use the web. Main advantages of the WWW, that make it attractive for use in education are the web's ease of use, the hypertext/hypermedia capability, the WWW networked basis, availability of client and server software for different platforms (mostly free of charge for non-commercial use), simplicity of HTML, and availability of free editing tools. In addition to the above characteristics, we have interactivity through the use of fill-out forms—input fields filled by users the content of which is sent to the server for further processing. In this way a user is more active than when he was only given ability to "click" on hyperlinks in documents. The most important characteristic of the WWW as a learning tool is its publishing capability. Even merely browsing through the WWW represents a form of learning, the so called "accidental learning"—"learning that happens at an unexpected moment, about an unexpected subject." However, there are more structured models of use of the WWW in education.

In spite of all positive aspects of the WWW, one needs to keep in mind possible negative effects of the WWW. Due to a multitude of contents offered on the web today, without a guidance to specific learning domains, a student can get lost in the "webspace" by finding pages that are interesting and entertaining, but do not contribute to learning. For this reason, it is important to stress the role of a teacher who directs students in using the WWW, but also encourages individuality in their work. To help teacher in this role, there are different search tools that help in finding information, or in information navigation. Due to the organisation of the WWW as a network service which works under the client-server model, the web is not only network service for searching and retrieving information but also for publishing information on internet. This yields two basic models of use of the WWW in education: information gathering, and publishing.

Information gathering

Gathering information that is offered on the internet though the WWW with the help of WWW clients or browsers represents the most common use of the WWW today. This includes accessing information available through other internet services (Gopher, e mail, Usenet News, Telnet, FTP, etc.), as well as those offered in hypermedia form by the WWW servers. The WWW and its browsers are more of a learning than a teaching tool because it is the student that controls the learning process of gathering information, and hence he is no longer a "passive learner".

When gathering information, it is important that the students not only learn how to locate information, but also what to do with it once they find it, that is how to transform information into knowledge. To achieve this, the teachers need to act as guides to students and help them put together a plan for information gathering. In the beginning it is necessary to practice information-gathering skills through simple exercises. For example, for a particular concept find a set of most relevant documents on the WWW that help explain the concept. Through this process the students learn to use different search engines and lists of resources. Once students learn this simple process of finding information, one can proceed with more complex projects in which the students answer given questions, explore different views on the same problem, solve real-world complex problems.

The use of the WWW for pedagogical purposes can develop in two basic directions:

1. use of the technology on a closed corpus of educational material, for the hypermedia and distance delivery capabilities of the web, and
2. use of this technology on an organised structure of links for an open corpus of material that was not necessarily meant initially for pedagogical use, but which can be "redirected" and exploited in guided educational explorations.

The first direction is similar to traditional distance learning approach. This includes, so called "hyper-courses" with the characteristics of ordinary courseware which is executed on a stand-alone machine, but with the advantage that it can be accessed via network from any location. In the second direction the materials searched are those published, not necessarily for educational use, on the web, and thus are not structured as in classic courseware.

In this way the students are more independent in their research, which in turn makes the role of a teacher as a guide that helps them find documents relevant for the given topic, as well as to stay away from pornographic and violence-related material, even more important. In this search one benefits from WWW search tools — search engines, and subject oriented catalogues of internet resources available on the WWW.

The biggest advantage of using the web in education is the ability to distribute educational multimedia presentations and courseware. The web supports two different techniques for distribution of courseware: distribution of complete software packages, and online browsing. In the first case, the entire package, created using an appropriate authoring tool for a specific platform, is downloaded via FTP. This is not so much different than distributing courseware on a diskette or a CD-ROM.

Online browsing refers to interactive browsing of courseware by specifying its URL using a WWW client. The advantages are that educational materials can be accessed, referenced, and re-used without limitations, which will, in the near future, create a universal educational environment that will change the philosophy of CAL. The most successful is the combination of the two methods, so that students use educational materials structured as classical courseware obtained by, or produced by the teacher, together with hyperlinks to documents related to a particular subject available on the internet. It is beneficial that the students themselves gather information, and structure it similarly to more traditional seminar papers, but not in the "paper", but rather in electronic form. This extends the use of the WWW from merely gathering information to publishing information.

Publishing

The simplicity of HTML for development of hypermedia applications allows that students not only learn hypermedia and searching the WWW, but also that they, themselves create their own projects. For example, instead of requiring students to present their findings about a given topic in form of a list of relevant URL's (e.g., bookmark file), one could ask them to create a homepage that incorporates found links, or a so-called synthetic document that synthesises the contents of other documents, references other documents and contains the student's analysis of the subject. Such documents help teachers determine which students did not complete the given research to a satisfactory level, and need additional help and more guidance in future assignments. If these documents are formatted as instructional hypermedia packages, they can serve other students for learning the subject, as well as examples for creating individual projects.

Teachers can use the WWW in education for development of courseware, where WWW browsers are used as GUI for the course-building environment. The advantages that courses are available using the internet and the WWW are: location and time independent delivery of course material, the ability to serve a large number of students at a potentially reduced cost, and a simple interface.

Both kinds of WWW use in education: information gathering and publishing, can be used in online, as well as in off-line mode. Information accessed online might be more recent and more varied in form compared to off-line information, but on the other hand, the advantages of the off-line mode of use is that it is not necessary to have a computer connected to the internet, but HTML documents should contain only local links and not to those resources located on other servers. In this case, either previously saved resources are searched on a hard disc or CD-ROM, or more often, educational hypermedia applications have characteristics of courseware that runs on a stand-alone machine. However, such HTML applications have an advantage over ones created by classical multimedia authoring tools, in that they can be easily made available to all on the internet by relocating them on a WWW server.

Other applications

In addition to above discussed basic uses of WWW in education, some authors give a more detailed classification. For example Carvin asserts that the WWW is used more in business and research, and to lesser extent in education, as a powerful educational tool. He gives four roles of the WWW in education: web as tutor, publishing tool, forum and navigator. The WWW as a tutor is used to present information clearly, attractively and practically using online hypermedia, and as such is useful for designing tutorials and lessons for a variety of subjects.

The web as a publishing tool enables students to create "hyper-reports" — online multimedia projects with links leading to numerous subtopics and network connections. Instead of classic seminars in which their work is presented in front of their peers and teachers, now the students present their work on the WWW in hypermedia form, and thus to a much larger audience. The web also encourages publishing of school online magazines and journals which motivates students' creativity and individual work.

The web is more and more used as a forum for discussions because of its user-friendly environment which not only enables easy use of Gopher and FTP services, but also reading of newsgroups, as well as sending and receiving e-mail. Using a listserv, one can also conduct virtual conferences — online discussions on a given topic where a website becomes an online forum and a successful combination of hypermedia presentation (the web) and critique (listserv, e mail). Studies have shown that some students are not comfortable expressing their opinions in front of a class, and their quietness is wrongly interpreted as lack of knowledge. This form of online communication using the network, enables such students to overcome their shyness and express their opinions to their colleagues.

The role of the web as a navigator is also important because it enables educators to find proper resources by the help of computerised search agents which will surf the internet looking for requested information, or catalogues which have listings of educational web sites. The web will begin to appear as a World-Wide Library Catalogue, but unlike a traditional library, the books that are available have been created by students and teachers.

Mosaic (a popular WWW browser) and the WWW are also successfully used by the special education teachers. Cossel Rice lists five uses of Mosaic: as a learning tool, tutorial, games one can create, whole language exercise, and library of supplemental curriculum materials. The first two uses are only adopted to the specific needs of students with development deficiencies. The use of games with an educational component, that are not for entertainment only, is particularly interesting for motivating students. Mosaic used for whole language exercises helps in work with students with reading and writing difficulties in that it motivates them to write something about themselves and their interests by creating their own home page, or by keeping a learning diary in which they write, in HTML form, what they have learned each day. It also helps teachers as a library of supplemental curriculum materials. When every school has its homepage with information on every class and every student, one will be able to speak of the "network of classrooms without walls".

An example of using the WWW for foreign language learning is WILT — A WWW based Interactive Language Teaching Tool developed at the University of Chicago. The WWW was chosen for the development of such system because it is easy to use, platform independent, and can be extended with new lessons and exercises in the future. Likewise, the use of fill-out forms enabled teachers to add and delete exercises from their homepages without the knowledge of HTML. It has been shown that WILT has an advantage over traditional teaching because it enables individualising of the learning process which is not present in traditional foreign language classrooms.

With a goal to explore how the WWW as a new technology can be used in education, North Dakota State University (NDSU) started the world wide web Instructional Project. The results of the study were published on a web server and include examples for preparing instructional materials in HTML, and a list of ready-to-use hypermedia courses stored on FTP servers at different universities, that can also be downloaded via FTP. Some of the courses contain an interactive component, that is they contain links to WWW servers with related content, so the newest information on the subject being studied is available to the students. Some instructors use the web to post homework and exam scores. The project was successful since both students and teachers have quickly accepted and learned to use the WWW in courses.

WWW is continuing its growth, and it is assumed that in future, it will assume even a greater role in commercial use, as well as in education. It is necessary to connect as many schools and universities to the WWW by creating websites, that is one needs to equip the schools and universities with necessary hardware and internet connections, and educate personnel that will maintain the server and provide help in using the new technology to the educators. It is to be expected that the development of new computer platforms and improvements in network bandwidth will enable a better quality use of the existing, as well as the development of new software that will allow easy access to the live discussions in a web environment, that will with the existing audio-visual capabilities further improve online education. Similarly, future additions to the HTML standards, especially new methods in the field of interactivity, such as CGI, Java applets, and virtual reality, will enable creation of even better and simpler interactive lessons for local and distant use.

Net-oriented Educational Projects

New methods and means are being used in countries around the world to improve education. In developed countries special attention is being paid to the role of computer technology in this process. Under consideration is the planned introduction of computer technology in education — not only in schools and universities, but also in corporations and homes.

Beside these global projects at government levels, there is a multitude of smaller projects involving often introduction of individual technologies, such as digital video, distance learning, multimedia, and networking, in individual schools and universities. While in some countries these efforts are strategically planned, in others, such projects represent isolated initiatives and more modest attempts which merely have a goal to build computer infrastructure and give schools and universities limited access to the internet.

Some examples of efforts to improve educational process by introduction of modern computer technology (primarily hypermedia and networking) are discussed below. Most of the examples come from the USA, Canada, Australia and Europe.

International Society for Technology in Education (ISTE)

ISTE is a non-profit professional organisation in USA dedicated to the improvement of education through computer-based technology, conforming to the requirements for education and training prepared by the National Coordinating Committee on Technology in Education and Training (NCC-TET). These requirements were developed in collaboration with US organisations representing education, training, government, defence, business, arts and cultural institutions, and libraries, and they would serve as guidelines to be used by the administration, congress, state agencies, national and state organisations, educational and training organisations to improve education primarily through the development of America's National Information Infrastructure (NII).

Main recommendation is to make NII accessible to all Americans in their homes and workplaces, as well as schools, institutions of higher education, libraries, and arts and cultural institutions. To achieve this goal it is necessary to develop education, training, and telecommunications applications, train teachers to use these applications and equipment, supply the technology and networking technologies in particular. Among others, activities of ISTE include publication of journals and guidebooks for teachers that help them learn about new technologies and how to use them. Other activities include starting mailing lists, conference organisation, and making recommendations on standards for use of technology in education.

Leading American experts in the field of education technology were involved in ISTE project "The Vision: TEST (Technologically Enriched Schools of Tomorrow)", the purpose of which was to provide educational decision makers with recommendations for improving schools. A study was made on current status in American K12 schools (included were 45 schools which had already successfully used technology) by interviewing teachers, students and administrators. Based on the study, recommendations were made for school restructuring required to make effective use of computer technology, and the following were the main conclusions:

> Technology can assist well-trained and well-equipped teachers to develop the intellectual potential of all their students.
>
> Technology, in the hands of trained teachers, is especially powerful when used with at-risk students.
>
> Teachers are the key to success in any educational change. They must be trained, supported, and provided with adequate resources in order to be successful in implementing new teaching methods.

KIDLINK

KIDLINK is the name of an organisation which, each year, leads KIDS-nn project (currently project KIDS-97 is underway until May 3, 1997). The goal of these projects is to involve as many children, ages 10-15, as possible in a global dialogue using internet. Since 1990, approximately 60,000 children from 87 countries from all of the continents have participated in these projects.

KIDLINK has several different forums for youth dialogue. Some support individual dialogue, while others support classroom dialogue. All KIDLINK youth participants begin with a personal introduction, after that they are free to participate in any KIDLINK youth dialogue projects: individual youth dialogue, dialogue for classroom youth, open topic, open inquiry, Japanese, Nordic, Portuguese or Spanish youth dialogue, organised youth discussion, special youth projects. Much of this dialogue is in words, but some youths choose to express themselves in graphic form. Besides e mail, the KIDLINK Internet Relay Chat (IRC) network is used for a real-time communication.

The Educational Resources Information Center (ERIC)

ERIC is an information system in the US that provides, through its 16 subject-specific clearinghouses and support components, a variety of services and products on education-related issues. As a part ERIC has AskERIC — an internet-based education information service, headquartered at the ERIC Clearinghouse on Information & Technology at Syracuse University.

AskERIC is composed of three major components: AskERIC Q & A (Question Answering) Service, AskERIC Virtual Library and AskERIC R&D (Research & Development). The Question Answering Service responds to questions on educational research, education issues, or the practice of education. The AskERIC Virtual Library is an internet site of selected resources for education and general interest (lesson plans, ERIC database, topical guides to internet, archives of education-related list servers, remote access to other internet sites) accessible via telnet, ftp, Gopher or WWW.

The research & development team uses the newest technology in instructional design, development and evaluation computer graphics design, hypermedia, organisation of information resources, programming, and network administration to improve the quality of AskERIC information services.

The Centre for Applied Research in Education (CARE)

CARE was founded in 1994 as department at the College of Education at the University of Texas with a goal to help research activities of schools, faculty and doctoral students in that part of the US. CARE maintains The Research Page through which professors, students and guests can access information on international online publications, school improvement networks and databases specialising in educational issues and topics. In addition, the Research Advisor provides guidance on educational research design and analysis for University of Texas students and faculty.

Web66

Web66 is a K12 project started at the University of Minnesota College of Education with a goal to introduce K12 teachers to the WWW as a "catalyst" that will integrate the internet into K12 schools. The goals of this project are:

1. To help K12 educators learn how to set up their own internet servers.
2. To link K12 WWW servers and the educators and students at those schools.
3. To help K12 educators find and use K12 appropriate resources on the WWW.

Hillside Elementary School was chosen as a pilot school for the Web66 project. Web66 project WWW server contains the list of all K12 schools registered on the network, information and news on WWW, as well as instructions for setting up a WWW server ("Web66 Classroom Internet Server Cookbook"), interconnecting schools ("Web66 Network Construction Set "), and creating HTML pages. The project also includes Web66 Mailing List, and the forum for the WebMaster.

Global Schoolhouse Project (GSH)

GSH lasted during 1993-94 connecting classrooms around the world in order to emphasise the potential of the internet, and in particular Mosaic (the most popular WWW browser at the time) for use in education. Within the project collaboration technologies, interfaces, and advanced information-retrieval tools were developed.

Technology Based Learning Network Canada (TBL.CA)

In Canada, since summer of 1994, the project called Technology Based Learning Network Canada (TBL.CA) has been actively pursued following the observation that a modern educational system is crucial for developing adaptability to changes in world economy, which is very important for Canadian economic future.

The goal of TBL.CA is to explore applications of technologies from animation and multimedia to interactive networked communications to fulfil students' needs in homes, schools, museums, the workplace and universities. To achieve this goal TBL.CA includes the following activities: "teach research and development skills in technology-based learning to hundreds of graduate students; provide opportunities for further study and professional development for research staff; support diverse technology-based learning opportunities in industry; educate teachers in the use of multimedia to integrate technology skills and information in their teaching; and provide future teachers with skills in the delivery of high quality technology-supported home schooling."

The Australian Society for Educational Technology (ASET)

In Australia, since 1975, the Australian Society for Educational Technology (ASET) is active as the national crganisation for people with professional interests in educational technology. ASET defines Educational Technology as "the design, development, implementation and evaluation of systems, methods and materials to achieve effective outcomes and improve the process of human learning." Similarly to American ISTE, ASET organises forum for discussion on educational technology issues, conferences, the emailing list edtech-aus, workshops, discussions and meetings, providing assistance and advice and publishing a quarterly newsletter, as well as the *Australian Journal of Educational Technology,* issues awards to stimulate production and applications of media and technologies in education and training.

*I*M EUROPE*

I*M EUROPE (Information Market - Europe) is an organisation which acts as a medium for supporting the actions of DGXIII of the European Commission in stimulating the European electronic information services market and multimedia content industries. Multimedia Educational Task Force was established to explore effects of technology, and in particular multimedia with a goal of improving education. The objectives of the Task Force are to make an analysis of the educational multimedia situation in schools and universities, as well as in the workplace and homes, and, based on the results, draw a plan to better utilise the technology in the future.

The field covered by the Task Force concerns educational and cultural products and services which can be accessed via television sets or computers, whether or not connected to telematics networks, used in the home, in educational and training institutions or at work, and offering a high level of interactivity.

Project of internet in school

Project Internet dla Szkol (Internet in School) has a goal to provide internet access for high schools in Poland and to teach students and teachers how to use internet services for communication (e-mail, Usenet, IRC) and for obtaining resources (ftp, WWW). The project also stimulates communication between Polish students with their colleagues from other countries, in order to exchange experiences and ideas, stimulates joint educational projects and contacts with academic staff to help students working on the net. At first Warsaw high schools, and later other schools in Poland were connected to Research and Academic Computer Network (NASK).

A similar project is Polish School on the web which is an attempt to build virtual Polish Schools on the web, which should allow children of Polish emigrants to learn and keep contact with the Polish language and culture. Younger children (ages 5-8), used to playing computer games, in a similar environment using the WWW hypermedia application, could learn Polish language, history, culture and geography. Older children, on the other hand, could also practice their writing skills by writing e-mail messages (within WWW forums) to teachers in Poland.

Universal Access to School Networking

During the last few years, thousands of schools and hundreds of thousands of students and teachers have begun to develop the internet into a major educational resource. Within the community of educational researchers, the internet is now an accepted standard. Network use is also growing rapidly throughout the larger educational community, but several factors have placed practical limits on this growth. The reasons that propel educational use of the internet include the following:

i) *Isolation:* Wide-area computer networks can help end the isolation of students and teachers in the traditional classroom. Of course, networks will accomplish this end only if they are inexpensive enough to be made available to all students and teachers.

ii) *Equity:* Connecting all schools to the internet will provide equity of access to online information and create opportunities for all schools to publish online. This requires a reasonably priced infrastructure that all schools can afford to purchase, install, and maintain.

iii) *Reform:* Networks can be a powerful tool in support of educational reform. A widespread network infrastructure with easy access to information servers and tools for placing resources on servers will allow students, classes, and teachers to produce online materials, do extensive collaborative work, and broadly share instructional resources.

Schools face possible obstacles in each of these areas. If a school cannot obtain adequate connectivity, its ability to overcome isolation will be limited. If it has no access to a server, its ability to publish materials online will be limited. If it has too few user devices for all students to participate in networking activities, the promise of equity will not be achieved. And if tools do not exist that enable students and teachers to use networks imaginatively and effectively to support their broader educational goals, the promise of educational reform will not be met. Overcoming each of these obstacles entails a technological challenge.

Shared Infrastructure

Networking is a means of building community, and a strong sense of community is often the key to building viable network-linked educational programmes and resources and sustaining them over the long term. The types of educational and community networks differ in some essential ways from those developed for many commercial applications.

Commercial networks emphasise privacy and security issues over cost and access considerations. For educational and community networks, cost and access are the primary concerns, and network architectures that neglect these factors are unlikely to be sustainable for very long.

Shared infrastructure and broad applicability bring other educational benefits. They create network environments that are conducive to interdisciplinary and collaborative activities and to research projects that explore an ever-expanding scope of resources. These sorts of activities and projects can contribute effectively to educational reform.

The portions of networks with the highest development costs and the greatest need for cost reduction are precisely those with the fewest possibilities for shared infrastructure. To put the issue in colloquial terms, we must deal not so much with the problem of building the information superhighway as with building the information driveway that leads into the home or classroom. Once this part of network connectivity is established, there remains the task of using it effectively to access online material and produce materials for others to use.

Performance and Affordability of Internetworking

The factors dramatically affect the performance and affordability of internetworking are the cost and bandwidth of the "local loop" from the user's site to the nearest network point of presence, and the existence of a complementary wide-area infrastructure to tie the various local loops together. These two factors are critical regardless of the specific details of the chosen technology or the market position of the service provider.

Schools and communities should choose their network technologies and services strategically, with an eye toward how their choices will support and leverage the overall networking infrastructure. Broad infrastructure needs are a much more important consideration in developing educational and community networks than in planning private networks or networks that serve a limited number of public or non-profit organisations.

Even though educational programmes have a specific focus, they inspire other activities, and they rely on other organisations for many kinds of resources. Hence, it is important to consider the entire community as a unit when assessing alternatives for providing an economical infrastructure for school or community networking.

First, let us take up the issue of providing the local loop. Several factors make it likely that the costs of providing connectivity will drop, perhaps dramatically, in the next few years. One strong influence is market competition to supply the local loop. Where there are multiple suppliers of connectivity to schools, homes, or offices, competitive forces will help reduce the cost of network services to these sites.

Many communities are experiencing active competition in this area, although recent federal telecommunications legislation may allow the re-establishment of monopolies of local connectivity, with a corresponding decrease in options and likely increase in price. One must also take care to distinguish competition in the local loop from competition in limited market segments, such as voice or video services. While this latter form of competition could decrease the price of specific services, it may have no relevance to data services and internetworking. More typically, some service providers may engage in "cream-skimming"—seeking to exploit market segments with the highest profit margins, a practice which public utility commissions and local regulatory authorities should probably discourage.

Tariff policies also affect the viability of various options for internet access. For example, the commonly available digital telephone service known as ISDN can provide economical connectivity at moderate bandwidths, as long as its tariffs are set at an affordable flat rate. When time charges are applied, this service becomes uneconomical for typical network interconnects, since it is desirable to keep the connection in place throughout the day.

Competition to provide local loops is likely to involve a number of new technologies. Telephone subscribers can employ new electronics—most notably, a technology known in telephonic circles as High-bit-rate Digital Subscriber Loop

(HDSL)—to wring vastly higher data rates out of older copper infrastructure. HDSL can provide data services at speeds in excess of one megabit per second and costs as low as one-tenth those of traditional connections.

Public utility commissions will ultimately determine whether these economies result in savings for home, school, and office subscribers or in larger profits for telephone companies. This is a complex issue, since rates are determined not only by the intrinsic cost of any single service to the telephone company, but also by the fraction of equipment and maintenance left in the hands of the customer, the need to subsidise certain lifeline services, and the need to average rates across the many different technologies used to supply local loops for a given region.

In addition to HDSL, which provides a symmetrical service, there are also asymmetrical services, such as Asymmetric Digital Subscriber Loop (ADSL). Symmetrical services provide the same data rate into and out of a given site. Asymmetrical services typically provide higher data rates into a given site than out of it. While asymmetrical services may be acceptable for a residence, where the users are mostly consumers of information, they would not be appropriate for connections to local area networks at schools and libraries because they would limit the ability to publish information at these sites.

Although some ADSL technologies have much higher bandwidths than HDSL, they provide significantly higher speeds only in the forward (outward) direction, and they cannot drive data for the distances that HDSL can. A new service known as SDSL promises to offer the bandwidth advantages of ADSL in a symmetrical mode.

Another promising development in the field of telephony is the deployment of fibre optics, either to drop points in the neighbourhood or to the curbside of subscriber homes or offices. Fiber brings vastly higher bandwidth than copper and promises higher reliability over time. Once the capital costs of laying this new infrastructure are depreciated, suppliers can anticipate significant reductions in the costs of providing high-bandwidth data services, namely, those with speeds in excess of 1 million bits per second. Such services would exhaust only a tiny fraction of the bandwidth available through a fibre infrastructure, which can also provide video services requiring the equivalent of tens of millions of bits per second.

Some telephone companies are contemplating a fibre optic/coaxial cable hybrid system, an architecture commonly used by newer cable television installations. These systems provide a particularly attractive architecture for data services and internetworking: they can offer services with peak bandwidths of 10 to 40 million bits per second or higher, at prices potentially competitive with those of present-day analog telephone service.

Widespread deployment of such systems will help redefine the pricing structure for high-bandwidth data services, as prices drop as low as a few percent of current service offerings. With extensive deployment, the cable modems needed to deliver this service can be marketed at prices comparable to those of conventional modems, and the service itself can be sold for prices comparable to those of premium cable channels.

Where internal wiring is costly to install and where external connectivity is difficult to achieve through fixed links, wireless technologies offer an attractive option. With its ease of setup, wireless is particularly appealing in situations where costly and time-consuming building modifications are necessary to install internal wiring. Wireless links can also be used to provide pieces of a metropolitan area network infrastructure.

But one must bear in mind that maintenance costs for wireless links are likely to be higher than those for fixed wiring and that the bandwidth available for wireless communications is extremely limited compared to the bandwidth of fixed copper or fiber infrastructure. This important point has been largely overlooked by groups advocating wireless technologies as a panacea for public network access. These technologies offer an excellent starting point for such access, but as usage grows, the bandwidth available through this medium will inevitably become saturated, and the majority of public internet traffic will have to be transferred to traditional fixed communications links. Thus, there will have to be truly compelling reasons to deploy wireless communications between fixed points in a metropolitan area.

Wireless technologies can be used effectively, however, as a rapid enabler, a temporary connection that can serve a networking purpose while fixed wiring is being planned and installed. Upon completion of wiring, the wireless apparatus might be reused to help leverage another start-up site.

New technologies are also generating new means of tying together local loops to form a wide-area networking infrastructure. New telephone architectures offer the possibility of significantly reduced costs for data services and internetworking. The traditional telephone infrastructure connects lines from homes and offices to switches at the telephone company's central offices, forming circuits through which telephone calls are routed. This circuit-switched infrastructure is oriented toward point-to-point connections, with endpoints that may be very widely separated. Each connection ties up switch and transmission resources for the duration of the connection, regardless of how much information is being passed through the circuit.

Internet services are based upon a quite different architecture, one that involves a common "cloud" of connectivity through which individual data packets are routed to their final destinations. This packet-switched infrastructure offers a number of significant advantages for data transmission. Individual circuits need not be maintained, so there are lower costs in terms of switches and infrastructure relating to the transmission plant. Demands are made upon this infrastructure only during the actual transmission of data packets.

Furthermore, the system can be overloaded briefly with only a slowdown in the rate of data transmission as opposed to a failure to establish a desired connection. This type of packet-switched infrastructure can be provided through a number of technologies commonly offered by the telephone industry and referred to collectively as "fast packet services".

The optimal mix of technologies will depend upon local pricing and needs. More important than specific programmatic needs may be the overall strategies employed to provide connectivity to schools and community centres in a given area.

The following points are relevant for schools and communities developing strategies for connectivity:

i) *Local points of presence:* Nearby access to the internet cloud lowers the cost of the local loop by reducing the need for long distance or local measured calls. Ideally, any telephone company central office should provide an entry point to the internet. This is likely to be a very cost-effective mechanism for the commodity provision of internet access.

ii) *Shared infrastructure.* Possibilities for shared infrastructure include shared bandwidth for links among central offices, shared modem pools for dial-up connectivity, and shared points of public access.

iii) *Local aggregation of traffic.* School districts can aggregate traffic and purchase bulk connectivity to pass this traffic to the internet cloud. Municipal governments can play a similar role for community centres and government offices. These groups assume a portion of the responsibility for network management and thereby reduce costs for the end users.

Effective Use of Connectivity

Together with connectivity, the quality of information available over the network and the ability of schools and communities to use the network as their own publishing venue are also important to create a networked environment of value to schools and communities.

The content challenge involves a set of technical issues and a number of social issues. The social issues relate to the evolution of the network community, the formation of networked collaborations, and the financing of network resources that exploit the full richness and depth of the medium. Technological factors can assist in these areas, but human factors ultimately will determine the network's success and relevance.

The architecture of low-cost online services is increasingly dominated by client/server mechanisms for delivering information. Determining the costs of such services requires an analysis of the costs of the client and server machines and the availability of software suitable to provide these services. Let us consider the question of client machines or access devices. Computers can be bought now for $1,000 to $2,000. This has been true for the last half-dozen years, and it is likely to remain true as long as the only forces governing these prices are traditional computer marketplace forces.

It is not the price of the raw materials or the manufacturing cost that determines the retail price of personal computers. Rather, marketing strategies and advertising decisions set these prices. Producing a $200 user device capable of running a web browser over standard telephone links is within the realm of possibility, provided that a large enough market exists for such a device. Many forces are converging to make it likely that such devices will be produced. These include the progress of game machines, which now typically contain powerful graphics computers as a standard component, the development of set-top boxes for cable television systems, and the need of schools for large numbers of cheap, networked computers.

With the evolution of computer hardware, operating systems, and software, it is possible to pass still-serviceable hardware from business and government offices into the hands of schools and community groups, who could use it to gain basic internet access at extremely low cost. The advent of Windows 95, with its significant new hardware demands, is beginning to drive many commercial users to invest in new hardware. But much of the remaindered hardware is still capable of running the older Windows operating system and supporting graphical interfaces to internet resources.

If commercial users donated remaindered hardware to schools and community centers, and if mechanisms to support this hardware were put in place, it might be possible to rapidly provide network access to all of the nation's classrooms. There are many uncertainties associated with such a scheme. It assumes that the evolution of software for classroom application will be much slower than the evolution of commercial software, so that the Windows machines will be adequate for most educational applications for a number of years. And it assumes that new features in commercial software will not make the training that students receive with older machines and software irrelevant to the commercial workplace. Finally, it assumes that older machines can be supplied in quantities sufficient to provide school districts with a uniform and supportable computing environment.

If these conditions can be met, the donation of older equipment could provide a significant boost to school and community networking efforts. This is only an interim approach and a partial solution for school and community networking, but it should allow communities to stretch significantly the dollars available for networking projects.

Whether the client machines are standard office computers or low-cost school and home computers, they will require affordable client software in order to access common information services. Under one widely used marketing model that works to the advantage of educational users, software vendors charge a fee for their server software but give away client software free of charge to all users or, more commonly, to educational users.

The rationale for this pricing model is that it encourages access to online information, for which there may be an access fee. Vendors may also charge a fee for the construction of servers to groups that place information online for commercial access. Under this type of pricing arrangement, it is possible for educational users to obtain high quality web and Geographical Information System browsers, among others. The practical consequence is that the client code is free to educational users but is well-maintained to insure the availability of solid code for all commercial clients.

Whether the market will continue to support this type of pricing structure depends largely on whether the majority of vendors adhere to standards for transporting information over the network. If large volumes of material are available through a small set of common standard protocols, there are likely to be low-cost or free products available to implement these standards. If one vendor obtains a near monopoly on the market, there is a danger of that vendor introducing proprietary protocols in its products and forcing educational users to purchase them at arbitrarily high prices. We would regard this as a classic monopoly situation that could be addressed under existing anti-trust laws.

On the server side, there is a relatively broad range of options, consistent with the idea that one need support only a small set of network protocols to supply a very wide range of information services. With an increasing number of vendors supplying internet servers for school use, we are fast approaching the possibility of a generic internet server. Generic servers can be built on the most common hardware platforms with public domain operating systems at a fraction of the cost of servers commonly available just a year or two ago.

Current networking projects and forthcoming network products are likely to produce enough examples of server set-up and maintenance to make their operation practical in any school or school district. Further simplification of this task will occur as new software is developed to facilitate the management of these machines, both locally at the school site and remotely from a district office or contracted system management provider.

Some vendors provide free client software but extract a fee, sometimes a very large one, for the server software. Fortunately, many vendors are adjusting server charges based on the features offered and the audience likely to use them. For example, systems that include advanced security features for financial transactions are likely to be sold at higher prices than systems meant for simpler information delivery systems. Here, too, adherence to a small set of network protocols makes it likely that low-cost or free implementation of information services will be available to educational and community networks.

The web services have their limitations, too, and to consider mechanisms that will help overcome these limitations for educational and community users. For example, the Java servers developed by Sun Microsystems can surmount some of the limitations of the hypertext markup language that forms the basis of the web. Java allows a server to pass new mini- applications to the client machine. Because these applications can be of greater complexity than standard web pages and because they are not limited by the constraints of the hypertext transfer protocol that underlies all web pages, the Java mechanism greatly expands the functionality of the web environment. We expect similar developments to continue to enhance server software and improve environments for developing and presenting online multimedia materials.

Construction of Digital Communities

Innovations in information technologies are interacting with new educational practices to bring about significant changes in human experience. Around the world, a remarkably ubiquitous educational system works well for some and poorly for others. Its elitism and class bias is global, a structural feature of the educational system built over the past four centuries. Educators designed the traditional system to make optimal use of a powerful information technology, that of printed text.

Digital technologies are for education as iron and steel girders, reinforced concrete, plate glass, elevators, central heating, and air conditioning were for architecture. Digital technologies set in abeyance significant, long-lasting limits on educational activity. Traditionally, the school and the classroom have been places where teachers and students are isolated from the general culture and where information and ideas have been relatively scarce — the textbook is a meager selection of what a field of knowledge comprises, a skilled teacher is a bundle of ignorance relative to the sum of learning, and a school library a sparse collection at best.

Networks reaching through the school into the classroom and to the desktop are ending the isolation and substituting a rule of abundance for that of scarcity. Such a new rule is not without its pitfalls, but to cope with these we must recognise that it is a new rule, deeply different from the old. Today, the educational problem changes profoundly, shifting from determining strategies for disbursing scarce knowledge to finding ways to enable people to use unlimited access to the resources of our cultures.

Multimedia, and its extension in virtual reality, is not merely a glitzy vehicle for edutainment hype. It is an epistemologically interesting development in our culture. For the most part, the work of thought has seemed to take place primarily through the manipulation of language, with the formal symbolisation of mathematics and logic seen as extensions of more everyday linguistic forms. Multimedia make it increasingly evident that the work of thinking can take many forms — verbal, visual, auditory, kinetic, and blends of all and each. Of course, nonlinguistic media are not new, but their status as serious means for creating knowledge is rising considerably.

Knowledge consists primarily of cultural resources that people can store and retrieve on demand, as the need for it arises. Written, especially printed, media long held a privileged place in education because they were easy to store and retrieve to suit the needs of users. Work in other media tended to exist in performances and monuments, which did not suit the strategies of random access. Multimedia changes that condition. It subjects a far wider range of communications to the full rule of random access, changing the repertoire of resources that people can store and retrieve effectively and use on demand to serve the needs of disciplined thought and inquiry.

People can use digital media both to acquire ideas and to express their thoughts in diverse ways. As a result, educators will find it increasingly difficult to favour the linguistic modality over all others, and they will need to broaden the norms of academic excellence. Digital technologies expand personal potentialities. Distributed processing and ubiquitous computing may or may not aggregate into artificial intelligence in the strong sense, creating a species of machines that think in a significant way. But they are clearly coming to function as a means for augmenting our human intellectual skills.

Word processors warn of anomalous spellings as they occur; spreadsheets allow anyone to perform complex calculations quickly and accurately; and databases permit those with good memory or bad to manage information sets that neither could handle on his own. All sorts of more specialised tools greatly lower the skill levels needed to participate effectively in wide ranges of cultural activity. Precision and exactness may become trivial proficiencies because getting it right will be easy, provided one doesn't get it wildly wrong through some accidental error. With regard to such accidental but sometimes very portentous error, the ability to estimate and guess results, traditionally an educationally suspect knack, becomes an increasingly prized skill. Thus, educators are sensing that changes in information technologies can deeply transform the hallmarks of having acquired a decent education.

Digital libraries, multimedia, and augmented skills change the limits of educational practice. The basic proposition here is not so much a normative argument that educators should, for one or another reason, accept that these three developments are empowering the transformation of educational activity. As educators experience changing conditions of communication in their work, they understand that these developments are profoundly altering the spectrum of pedagogical possibility.

This new conditions open the educational system to significant change. The new conditions, however, do not determine what will emerge. Educators are determining what emerges through the social construction of digital learning communities. Educational structures from kindergarten through graduate schools and adult education are increasingly in flux. Structures are wrenching open to change; but the course that change can and should take must be determined through the interplay of effort by many different groups.

Individual educators may or may not welcome that condition, but critic and evangelist alike sense that the new conditions open the educational system to significant change. The new conditions, however, do not determine what will emerge. Educators are determining what emerges through the social construction of digital learning communities. Educational structures from kindergarten through graduate schools and adult education are increasingly in flux. Structures are wrenching open to change; but the course that change can and should take must be determined through the interplay of effort by many different groups.

New information technologies are opening the system to new possibilities as surely as new building technologies did to architecture some hundred years ago. People, acting in the face of uncertainty, must determine what they can make of these emerging possibilities. Many groups and interests, pursuing many divergent inspirations, are vying for command, and a kaleidoscope of coalitions establishes, through diverse initiatives, emerging norms of practice.

Many in journalism and commerce avidly attend to the entertainment industries as potential sources of educational innovation. They may be right in viewing practitioners of edutainment—the merger of education and entertainment in products, at once enlightening and engaging, to be marketed to both homes and schools—as the key groups that determine emerging pedagogical prospects. Certainly, a great deal of commercial capital currently drives efforts to develop edutainment products, and there are powerful channels of distribution available to reach the public.

Significant limitations to these efforts to restructure educational practice through edutainment are at work, however. Edutainment's stuff in trade is a set of products to be sold in the educational markets of home and school. Indubitably, schools and teachers and students, engaged in the work of education, constitute a market for the sale of various goods—food, books, clothes, pens and pencils, furniture, fuel oil, rings, electronics, and software. Education as such, however, is not inherently a market, with success measured in market share and relative efficiency in making and distributing product.

As a human phenomenon, education is not a market for products, but a process of growth and transformation, one sustained over many years with success measured throughout the vicissitudes of personal and collective experience. Indeed, many companies may do well by doing good. But producers of edutainment have yet to show whether they have either an interest in the human process of education or the capacity to give it intentional shape.

Overcoming decades, the prime movers of educational innovation are more likely to be the knowledge industries and intellectual institutions, which are already the prime locus of education. Education is the work of educators, not movie producers, broadcasters, or theme-park operators. Educational institutions—schools, universities, museums, laboratories, libraries—are the major factors in the social construction of a new educational system. Worldwide they control a huge annual cash flow, derived from individual, governmental, philanthropic, and commercial sources, a cash flow more than sufficient to underwrite far-flung innovation. Furthermore, they control and produce intellectual property of extraordinary breadth and depth.

Across every field, education included, people need both pure scholarship and professional learning. If, from the perspective of intellectual institutions, a spectrum running from pure to applied, from academic to professional, characterises knowledge, then a gradient running from theory to policy to practice generally describes the intellectual and educational uses to which people put that knowledge.

As educators increasingly work with the new technologies in the extended present, they experience a basic that runs counter to the pessimistic view, at once so weary and wary. Current innovations insinuate into daily circumstances the grounds for recognising that the relevant agencies of action are not finite and fixed. The new information technologies provide powerful, underutilised tools for pursuing the ideals of universal education and the right of all to engage as equals in the common pursuit of life, liberty, and happiness.

Engaged with emerging possibilities, people who are working to apply digital technologies to education experience a sense of historical empowerment; they assert views about the value of their effort to improve the character of the human enterprise, namely, the view that people can and should use these new tools of communication to carry the work of enlightenment forward to unprecedented levels of fulfilment.

In this experiential world, digital technologies are an expression of the power of reason in human life, making plausible the hope and expectation that reason is still becoming an evermore effective asset in the service of human life. Educators are far from having made their mission obsolete, and the digital technologies provide an important new means to advance towards unfinished enlightenment aspirations.

Educators working with the new technologies command powerful tools, historically significant tools. Educators need to look beyond the myopic topic of computers in education to the question of what they can and should accomplish as educators making full use of digital tools. Educators should use these wonderfully powerful tools to pursue historically challenging goals—fulfilling basic human rights; securing the physical well-being of all in a sustainable global environment; eliminating prejudice, poverty, despair, and disease.

In the social construction of a new educational system, educators need to possess and to impart principles suitable for determining intentions in a world in which the instruments of action are global, complex, and massive in effects. Our world is the posterity of people who pursued demanding visions, initiating a rule of law, industrial production, systematic science, effective medicine, universal schooling. They asserted these possibilities often while living under atrocious conditions, and the measures of dignity, comfort, and well-being that we enjoy derive largely from their efforts. But that well-being is neither stable nor universal.

To construct a new educational system, educators need to engage the great problems and opportunities of the extended present with substantial, epochal effort. Through the foreseeable future, on the local, national, and global scale, economic inequality and cultural differences will persist, fomenting resentment and fear, misunderstanding and hostility, while even the lone extremist can wield weapons that challenge the stability of societies and states.

Throughout the history of educational efforts until the current juncture, the problem of policy has been to deploy and allocate scarce information and educative resources. Educational policy as it has existed has been a complicated system for allocating differential access to the cultural assets of the world's civilisations and for legitimating the results. Soon, educational policy will need to be redefined to take into account a completely novel starting point—all the resources of the world's cultures will in principle be available to any person at any place at any time.

In many different ways, traditional educational policy has served to allocate scarce resources so that preferential access will benefit society and seem legitimate to its members. Policy issues have turned on a fundamental trade-off between people and cultural resources. Under a regime of scarcity, educational institutions can avail a narrow selection of the culture to all people and a full representation of it to a few. In every polity and society throughout the world, formal educational systems consist of pyramidal structures in which very large cohorts receive instruction in basic subjects—reading, writing, and arithmetic.

The whole structure of educational opportunity necessarily identified and prepared a limited number who could make optimum use of the exhaustive resources while endowing others, in due measure, with lesser educational opportunities correlated to their aptitude and need.

A movement from the pole of constraint towards its opposite is having profound effects on the formation of curricula. Traditionally, curricular resources in schools represent highly constrained choices, and policies determining who teaches what to whom, the methods they use, and the means for assessing the performances of students, teachers, and schools all serve to manage and legitimate these constraints. These policies result in tenaciously ridiculous judgments of cultural worth, as educators have had to rationalise a cramped canon and a sample of historical interpretations that have been simplified to the point of stupidity.

In field after field, the range of cultural resources that have substantial educative worth has far exceeded what publishers could cram into textbooks or schools could purchase for their libraries. Thus, the great paradox arose that, except at its most elite pinnacles, education has been a consistently anti-intellectual profession.

Throughout the era of scarce educative resources, the basic problem of practice has been to make these scarce resources stretch as far as possible. The basic strategy has been the strategy of instruction, which requires large numbers of children to learn in unison. This strategy has been in force for centuries. It is the strategy that accounted for the design of schools, the workings of classroom practice, the organisation of the day and year, the plan of the curriculum, and the function of textbooks. Under a regime of cultural affluence, the effort to make a few cultural resources stretch as far as possible makes little sense.

Inquiry, study, problem solving can become the prime educational activities in a system making full use of digital resources. Educators have often commended these as the best modes of learning, but despite numerous reform efforts, practice always seemed to revert to norms of traditional instruction. Digital resources represent a powerful investment in the power of the student to inquire and to learn. Given effective tools of access, analysis, simulation, and synthesis, students can accomplish many things with these resources that they could not do without them. As a result of empowering students more effectively, what teachers need to do to help students develop knowledge, character, and skill changes as well. These shifts require a difficult change in mindset about the process of education.

Thereafter educators become far more paternalistic, and generally assume that children cannot exercise wise judgment about their own education. The cost of this assumption is a frequent estrangement of students from their education. As digital resources become the infrastructure for education, it becomes much more feasible to test whether or not paternalistic efforts to accelerate the pace of learning are, in fact, counterproductive and whether both time and value can be gained by ceasing to understand the business of the student as learning what teachers teach and instead recognising it as doing what their name suggests—studying those things that the student finds significant.

In a new educational system, centering initiative and control with the student is a fundamental principle of design and a measure of good practice. The role of teachers remains great: it is the role of fomenting questions, doubts, uncertainties; modelling strategies of inquiry; and criticising the quality of results. Curriculum design becomes the art of posing problems and facilitating work upon them. As educators adapt work to empower the student, they will create settings in which:

i) Students will work primarily in small collaborative groups on challenging projects that take a significant period of time to complete and cut across normal disciplinary boundaries.

ii) Students will have access to digital representations of nearly unlimited sources and data—documents, images, recordings, videos, maps, statistics, artifacts, monuments, and so on.

iii) Students can make effective use of digital tools that enable them to conduct sophisticated analyses, syntheses, and simulations—in other words, to perform work that is much closer in scope and quality to that of advanced scholars.

The transformation of education taking place is not a function of increased access to information. It is a function of increased *participation* in intellectual work—in advancing knowledge, applying skill, exercising judgment.

REFERENCES

Burns, Richard W., Gary D. Brooks (eds.), *Curriculum Design in a Changing Society*, Educational Technology Publications, Englewood Cliffs, NJ, 1970

Hardin, Joseph, John Ziebarth, *Digital Technology and its Impact on Education*.

Hiltz, S. R., *The Virtual Classroom: Initial Explorations of Computer-mediated Communication Systems as an Interactive Learning Space*, Newark, NJ: New Jersey Institute of Technology, 1985.

Kern, Richard, and Mark Warschauer, *Introduction: Theory and Practice of Network-Based Language Teaching*.

Klemm W. R., and Snell, J. R., "Enriching Computer-Mediated Group Learning by Coupling Constructivism with Collaborative Learning", *Journal of Instructional Science and Technology*, 1, No2, 1996.

Kerr, E. Hiltz, S., *Computer-Based Instruction*, 17(1), 1982

Martin, B. L., "Using Distance Education to Teach Instructional Design to Preservice Teachers", *Educational Technology*, Vol. XXXIV, No. 3, March 1994.

Rai, Amar Nath, *Distance Education: Open Learning Vs. Virtual University Concepts*, Authorspress, New Delhi, 2000.

Talesra, Hemlatha, Marashdeb and Nagda, *Web-Based Learning*, Authorspress, 2003.

Bibliography

Amadio, M., "Two decades of bilingual education", *Prospects,* UNESCO, Paris, vol. XX, no. 3, 1990, p. 343-41.

Anderson, L.M. and Ching, M., *Affective Teacher Education: International Encyclopaedia of Teaching and Teacher Education*, Pergamon Press, New York, 1987.

Armitage, S, and Steeples, C., "Guidelines for Using Computer Conferencing in Teaching", *BT CMC in HE Newsletter*, Issue 4,1996.

Baily, M., "Great expectations: PCs and productivity," In: R. Kling (editor). *Computerisation and Controversy.* San Diego: Academic Press, p. 21, 1996.

Barker, K., "Quality guidelines for online education and training", 12th April 2002

Barrows, H., *Practice-Based Learning: Problem-Based Learning Applied to Medical Education*, Springfield, Il: Southern Illinois University School of Medicine, 1994.

Bartolic, S. and Bates, A.W., "Investing in online learning: potential benefits and limitations", *Canadian Journal of Communication,* Vol. 24, No.3, 1999.

Bates, A.W, and Escamilla, J., "Crossing Boundaries: Making Global Distance Education a Reality", *Journal of Distance Education*, Vol.12, Nos. 1&2, pp. 49-66, 1997.

Bates, Tony, *Cultural and ethical issues in international distance education*", Director, Distance Education and Technology, Continuing Studies, The University of British Columbia

Bitter, G. G, Yohe, R. L., "Preparing teachers for the information age", *Educational Technology,* 29 (3), 22-25, 1989.

Boaz, Mary, et al., *Teaching at a Distance: A Handbook for Instructors*, Los Angeles, CA: League for Innovation in the Community

College and Archipelago, a Division of Harcourt Brace & Company, 1999.

Boettcher, Judith V, and Rita-Marie Conrad, *Faculty Guide for Moving Teaching and Learning to the Web*, Los Angeles, CA: League for Innovation in the Community College, p.16, 1999.

Bonk, C.J, & King, K.S., "Computer conferencing and collaborative writing tools: Starting a dialogue about student dialogue", In C.J. Bonk, & K.S. King (Eds.), *Electronic Collaborators: Learner-centered technologies for literacy, apprenticeship, and discourse*, Mahwah, NJ: Erlbaum, in press, 1998.

Boud, D., Felleti, G., *The Challenge of Problem-Based Learning*, London: Kogan, 1991.

Brookfield, S., *Becoming a Critically Reflective Teacher*, San Francisco: Jossey-Bass, p. 6, 1995.

Brown, A. L., "The advancement of learning", *Educational Researcher*, 23 (3), 4-12, 1994.

Brown, J., Collins, A.&Duguid, P., "Situated cognition and the culture of learning", *Educational Researcher*,18,32-42, 1989.

Burns, Richard W., Gary D. Brooks (eds.), *Curriculum Design in a Changing Society*, Educational Technology Publications, Englewood Cliffs, NJ, 1970

Catherine M, Gynn, Ph.D., "The Pedagogy of Technology Enhanced Learning Environments".

Chaurasia, Gulab, *Teacher Education and Professional Organisations*, Authorspress, New Delhi, 2000

Chickering, A.W., and Gamson, Z.F., "Applying the Seven Principles for Good Practice in Undergraduate Education, Fall 1991", San Francisco: Jossey-Bass Inc., *New Directions for Teaching and Learning*, 1991

Collins, M. et al., *Computer-Mediated Communication and the Online Classroom*, New Jersey, 1994.

Collis, B. et al., "Web Environments for Group-Based Project Work in Higher Education", *International Journal of Educational Telecommunications,AACE* 3.2 1997.

Crook, C., *Computers and the collaborative experience of learning*, Routledge: London & New York, 1994.

Dabbah, N., *Using a web-based course management tool to support face-to-face instruction*, 25 February 2002.

Dalton, D. W., "The effect of cooperative learning strategies on achievement and attitudes during interactive video", *Journal of Computer-Based Instruction*, 1990.

Dede, C., "Emerging technologies and distributed learning", *American Journal of Distance Education* 10, 2, 4-36, 1996.

Dillenbourg, P., et al. "Mediating the Mechanisms Which Make Collaborative Learning Sometimes Effective", *International Journal of Educational Telecommunications, AACE* 1.2, pp. 131-146, 1995.

Dubrovsky, V.J. et al, 'The Equalisation Phenomenon: Status Effects in Computer-Mediated and Face-to-Face Decision Making Groups", *Human Computer Interaction* 6, 1991.

Dwyer, Dan, Barbieri, Kathy, Doerr, Helen, "Creating a Virtual Classroom for Interactive Education on the Web", *The Third International World Wide Web Conference*, 1995.

Ferguson, T., "Communicating in the multilingual classroom", In: MacGregor, M., Moore, R., eds. *Tetrting mathematics in the multiculturul classroom : a resource for teachers and teacher educutors*, Melbourne, Australia, School of Science and Mathematics Education, Institute of Education, The University of Melbourne, 1991.

Gagne, R. M. and Briggs L., *Principles of Instructional Design.* Holt, Rinehart and Winston, New York, 1979.

Gibbons, A. S., & P. G., Fairweather, *Computer-based instruction: design and development*, Englewood Cliffs, NJ: Educational Technology Publications, 1998.

Gibbs, G., Pollard, N., Farrell, J., *Institutional Support for Resource Based Learning*, Oxford Centre for Staff Development, 1994.

Golas, K., "Guidelines for designing online learning", 12th April 2002.

Gorski, Paul, *Multicultural Education and the Internet: Tools, Resources, and Commentary*, Founder and Site Author of the Multicultural Pavilion, September,1999.

Goyal B.R., *Multigrade Teaching: In-service Education Package for Elementary Teacher Educators,* NCERT, New Delhi, 1992.

Graumann, C.F., "Commonality, mutuality, reciprocity: A conceptual introduction", In I. Markova, C. Graumann & K. Foppa (Eds.), *Mutualities in dialogue* (pp. 1-24), New York, Cambridge University Press, 1995.

Hafner, A.L., Spencer Green, J., "Multicultural education and diversity: providing information to teachers", Annual meeting of the American Association of Colleges of Teacher Education (San Antonio, TX), 1992

Hall, E.T., "Making sense without words", In: Fersh, S., ed. *Learning about peoples und cultures,* Evanston, McDougal, Litell, 1974.

Harasim, L. et al., *Learning Networks: A Field Guide to Teaching and Learning Online,* Cambridge, MA, 1995.

Hardin, Joseph, John Ziebarth, *Digital Technology and its Impact on Education.*

Heiner, Matthias, Schneckenberg, Dirk and Wildt, Johannes, "Online Pedagogy— Innovative Teaching and Learning Strategies in ICT-Environments" Background paper of the cevu workgroup Online Pedagogym 2001.

Herrington, A, Sparrow, H, Herrington, J., "Masters Online:Designing a university-wide curriculum development", In M.Wallace, A.Ellis, D.Newton, Eds., *Proceedings of the Moving Online Conference,* Lismore,NSW:Southern Cross University, 2000.

Herrington, Anthony, Bunker, Alison; "Quality teaching online:Putting pedagogy first" Edith Cowan University, Perth, Australia.

Herrington, J, Oliver, R., "An instructional design framework for authentic learning environments", *Educational Technology Research and Development,*48 (3), 23-48, 2000.

Hiltz, S. R., *The Virtual Classroom: Initial Explorations of Computer-mediated Communication Systems as an Interactive Learning Space*, Newark, NJ: New Jersey Institute of Technology, 1985.

Jonassen, D.H., *Computers in the Classroom: Mindtools for Critical Thinking,* Englewood Cliffs, NJ, 1996.

Jones, B., Valdez, G., Nowakowski, J., & Rasmussen, C., *Designing Learning and Technology for Educational Reform*, Oak Brook, IL: North Central Regional Educational Laboratory, 1994.

Jones, P., Jacobs, G., and Brown, S., "Learning Stylers and CAL Design: A Model for the Future", *Active Learning,* December 1997.

Kaufman, D., "Constructivist-based experiential learning in teacher education", *Action in Teacher Education* 18(2), 40-49, EJ 536 845, 1996.

Kern, Richard, and Mark Warschauer, *Introduction: Theory and Practice of Network-Based Language Teaching.*

Kerr, E. Hiltz, S., *Computer-Based Instruction*, 17(1), 1982

Kerry T, and Tollitt-Evans, J., *Teaching in Further Education*, Oxford: Blackwell, p. 120, 1990.

Khan, B.H., Ed., *Web-based instruction*, Englewood Cliffs, NJ: Educational Technology Publications, 1997.

Kiesler, S., Siegel, J. & McGuire, T.W., "Social psychological impacts of computer-mediated communication", *American Psychologist*, 39(10), 1123-1134, 1984.

Klemm W. R., and Snell, J. R., "Enriching Computer-Mediated Group Learning by Coupling Constructivism with Collaborative Learning", *Journal of Instructional Science and Technology*, 1, No2, 1996.

Koschmann, T.D., "Toward a theory of computer support for collaborative learning", *Journal of Learning Sciences*, 3(3), 219-225, 1994.

Kubala, Tom, "Addressing Student Needs: Teaching and Learning on the Internet", *THE Online Journal*, March 1998.

Kulik, J. A, and Kulik, C.L., "Effectiveness of Computer- based Instruction", *School Library Media Quarterly*, 17, 156-159, 1989.

Kurland, N. D., *Computer Communication: A New Tool for Distance Education*, Heerlen & Assen/Maastricht, 1986.

Lave, J, Wenger, E., *Situated learning: Legitimate peripheral participation*, Cambridge, UK: Cambridge University Press, 1990.

Lloyd, P. *Groupware in 21st Century: Computer Supported Co-operative Working Towards the Millennium*, Adamantine Press, 1994.

Martin, B. L., "Using Distance Education to Teach Instructional Design to Preservice Teachers", *Educational Technology*, Vol. XXXIV, No. 3, March 1994.

McConnell, D., *Implementing Computer Supported Co-operative Learning*, London, 1994.

McDiarmid, G.W., *What's the matter? Preparing teachers for culturally diverse classrooms*, Reno, NV, Far West Region Holmes Group, 1989.

Mendenhall, Robert W., *Technology: Creating New Models in Higher Education*, Western Governors University.

Merseth, K., "Supporting beginning teachers with computer networks", *Journal of Teacher Education*, 42, 140-147, 1991

O'Malley, C. ed., *Computer Supported Collaborative Learning*, Berlin, 1994.

Oliver, M., and Conole, G. "Evaluating Communication and Information Technologies: A Tookit for Practitioners", *Active Learning*, July, 1998.

Pachler, N., *Theories of Learning and ICT* ed. Marlyn Leask and Norbert Pachler, London: Routledge, 1999.

Pascarella, Ernest and Patrick Terenzini, *How College Affects Students*, San Francisco, CA: Jossey-Bass, 1991.

Patil, V.T, Dubey, S. N., *Inservice Education for Teachers,* Authorspress, New Delhi, 2001

Peters, Otto, *Teaching and Learning in Distance Education: Analysis and Interpretations from an International Perspective,* London: Kogan Page Limited, 1999.

Rai, Amar Nath, *Distance Education: Open Learning Vs. Virtual University Concepts*, Authorspress, New Delhi, 2000.

Rapaport, M., *Computer Mediated Communications,* New York, 1991.

Reigeluth, C. M., "Instructional design: What is it and why is it?", In C. M. Reigeluth (Ed.), *Instructional design theories and models: An overview of their current status*, Hillsdale, NJ: Lawrence Erlbaum Associates, 1983.

Rheingold, H., *Virtual Community: Homesteading on the Electronic Frontier*, Cambridge MA:MIT Press, 2000.

Schank, R. C., Berman, T. R., Macpherson, K. A., "Learning by doing", In C. M. Reigeluth (Ed.), *Instructional-design theories and models*, Volume II, 1999.

Scigliano J, and Levin, J., "One-stop shopping in an online educational mall," *T.H.E. (Technological Horizons in Education) Journal*, volume 27, number 11 June, 2000.

Shrum, L., "Introducing Teachers to Telecommunications: California's (ESTTI)," *T.H.E. (Technological Horizons in Education) Journal, volume 15,* number 8, April, 1998

South, J. B., Monson, D. W., "A university-wide system for creating, capturing, and delivering learning objects", In D. Wiley Ed., *The instructional use of learning objects*, Bloomington IN: Association for Educational Communications and Technology, 2002.

Steeples, C., et al, *Technological Support for Teaching and Learning: Computer-Mediated Communications in Higher Education,* Oxford, 1996.

Stepien, W.J. and Gallagher, S.A., "Problem-based Learning: As Authentic as it Gets", *Educational Leadership*. 50(7) 25-8, 1993.

Talesra, Hemlatha, Marashdeb and Nagda, *Web-Based Learning,* Authorspress, 2003.

Twining, "Planning to use ICT in schools?", *Education* 3-13, Vol 29, Issue 1, pp. 9-17, 2001.

Weiser, M., "The computer for the 21st century", *Scientific American* 265, 3, September, 1991.

Wells, R., "Computer-Mediated Communication for Distance Education: An International Review of Design, Teaching and